PRAISE FOR

"Easkey Britton asks us to dive [...] [...]d ourselves in the sea's echoing song – remi[...]ng [...] wh[...] w[...] [...] [...]e; what we hold the power to become. We need this book now more than ever. We need it's urgent, delicate truths; it's insistent call to action – for the good of the feminine, mothering, nourishing waters – and all we share them with."
Kerri ní Dochartaigh, bestselling author of *Thin Places*

"In this deeply empathic and practical handbook, scientist and surfer Easkey Britton distills her learnings to help us understand how water connects us all."
Bonnie Tsui, bestselling author of *Why We Swim*

"There is no better way to reconnect to the universal healing power of water than through stories – and there's no better storyteller than Easkey Britton. "
Dr Wallace J Nichols, *NYT* **bestselling author of** *Blue Mind*

"An evocative book that brings the water to you, and you to the water."
Dr Catherine Kelly, author of *Blue Places*

"Water is vital to our health, healing and wisdom. It's an essential part of what brings us alive. Thank you Easkey for this beautiful look at all that water is and can be."
Sarah Peck, founder of Startup Parent

"*Ebb & Flow* is a paean to the potency of water, from medicine to art, to geography and culture, and all points in between. This book will change your relationship with water forever."
Manchán Magan, bestselling author of *Listen to the Land Speak*

"Britton's wildly unique, yet inspiringly humble perspective as a professional surfer, social ecologist and artist challenges us all to mindfully redefine and passionately restore our connection to water, wellbeing and each other."
Dr Diz Glithero, PhD, National Lead at the Canadian Ocean Literacy Coalition

"In this book, Easkey brings the reader on a journey that is filled with wisdom, reminding us that water, the ocean and wellness are all interconnected."
Lea d'Auriol, founder of Oceanic Global

"Few writers have the extraordinary empathy and connection Easkey brings from her life spent getting wet in wild and wonderful ways"
Ed Gillespie, author of *Only Planet* and *Small Dreams of a Seahorse*

"Weaving together poignant threads of personal experience with diverse knowledges from around the world, *Ebb & Flow* moves us to reconsider the deeply reciprocal relationships between people and water. "
Dr Sarah Bell, senior lecturer in health geography, University of Exeter

"Sharing ancient wisdom for modern life, *Ebb & Flow* offers an experiential journey to reconnect to water, to ourselves and to life itself."
Pat Divilly, coach, podcaster and author of *Fit Mind*

"*Ebb & Flow* is a concise, reader-friendly page-turner that successfully integrates the scientific wisdom of Indigenous traditions, the voices of marginalized people, the latest in cutting-edge research and, of course, the author's own dynamic perspective. The result is a book that provokes awe, wonder and, despite the perilous situation, hope."
Prof Susan Prescott, MD, PhD, FRACP, Professor of Paediatrics at University of Western Australia, Director of the Nova Network

"In a time where it is so hard to find clarity around how to best care for our environment, *Ebb & Flow* reminds us that our hearts and senses can lead us to solutions and that our relationship should be intuitive and mutually nourishing. Rooted in tradition, respect, and introspection, this book is both comforting and motivating."
Connor Ryan, pro Lakota skier, activist and filmmaker

"Easkey's attunement with the open ocean is deep and purposeful, rich and wise, yet wonderfully gentle and always immediate. This outstanding new book goes beyond blue health to heal the heart, mind and body of our collective water planet."
Sam Bleakley, PhD, author of *Mindful Thoughts for Surfers*

"If you ever wondered how and why water makes you feel the way it does, this is a must read. Easkey does more than simply explain the importance of water, she reconnects us to it."
Cliff Kapono, PhD, professional surfer, ASU professor and journalist

"Packed with fascinating research and unique activities, this book will equip you to be a better steward of the sea."
Emma Loewe, author of *Return To Nature*

EBB & FLOW

Connect with the Patterns and Power of Water

Easkey Britton

WATKINS
1893

For Barra and Fianna, may water hold, heal and protect you always

Ebb and Flow
Easkey Britton

First published in the UK and USA in 2023
by Watkins, an imprint of Watkins Media Limited
Unit 11, Shepperton House, 83–93 Shepperton Road
London N1 3DF

enquiries@watkinspublishing.com

Publisher: Fiona Robertson
Assistant Editor: Brittany Willis
Head of Design: Karen Smith
Cover Designer: Kate Cromwell
Production: Uzma Taj

A CIP record for this book is available from the British Library

ISBN: 978-1-78678-646-3 (paperback)
ISBN: 978-1-78678-668-5 (eBook)

10 9 8 7 6 5 4 3 2 1

Typeset by Lapiz

Printed in the United Kingdom by TJ Books Ltd

www.watkinspublishing.com

CONTENTS

INTRODUCTION

When I began to write this book, *Ebb and Flow*, I didn't fully appreciate just how complex and entangled the human relationship with water is. How much we, our bodies and our actions, are a part of the water cycle. It is my hope that this book will offer the opportunity to reflect upon our personal relationship with water. How water is connected to our identity and places of origin, how it may remind us of our vulnerability as well as our vitality, and how we can all learn from water and its gift of cleansing and healing.

Ebb and Flow is an invitation to let go of certainties that you may have taken for granted. It is time to open yourself to different ways of being and belonging with water, by restoring and reimagining your watery entanglements through an ecological lens of interconnection and interdependence. Allow your renewed relationship with water to remake and reshape the rigid, dualistic "status quo", becoming more dynamic, fluid and cyclical, and challenge the conceit of humans who believe they are superior to the "wild".

Like the flow of the water cycle, renewing our relationship with water is a cyclical tale of rhythm and movement, giving and receiving, inhalation and exhalation, ebb and flow, where water is at the beginning and end of every cycle of life. Through this book, I hope that you will learn how and why you value water, what it means to you, and how it has shaped your cultural identity. I seek to share some of my own personal experience, shaped by the waters of my birth and my ancestors, of my place of belonging and its local, Indigenous and colonized histories.

Our understanding of water

Water is far more than purely an inanimate resource for human use and consumption. "Blue health"[1] is an emerging metadiscipline that seeks to explore and understand the relationship between human health and bodies of water, especially the mental and physical benefits of being in, on or near water. It helps us to understand how water makes us feel and its capacity to heal us.

As a social ecologist working in the area of blue health for the last decade, I have committed myself to better understanding humans' relationship with water, and in particular the impact of outdoor, natural or wild waters on our health and wellbeing. As environmental anthropologist Veronica Strang wrote in *Blue Space, Health and Wellbeing*, "We remain largely oblivious to flows of water in our bodies or, for that matter, in and through our cities, only becoming sharply aware of them when floods inundate the streets, or household taps fail to yield water supplies."[2]

Across cultures, especially Indigenous cultures, maintaining the flow of water has always been crucial to the maintenance of social, spiritual and environmental health. The understanding of water's effect on our psychological wellbeing reached more mainstream, popular consciousness following the 2014 publication of Wallace J Nichols book, *Blue Mind*, about the emerging science behind why water makes us feel happier, healthier and more connected. There is now a growing realization in modern society that water "holds the key to our health and we hold the key to the health of water".[3]

I have worked on national and international research projects seeking to understand and evidence the impact of water environments, or "blue spaces", on our health, especially our mental health and water's therapeutic benefits. This has included the nationally funded Nature and Environment to Attain and Restore (NEAR) Health project, the Seas, Oceans & Public Health in Europe (SOPHIE) project and INCLUSEA projects funded by the European Union. Although I was excited to be able to work in this emerging field, something about the blue health narrative began to sit uneasily with me. There was often the acknowledgement that our understanding of water as healing is nothing new, and how this belief can be found across cultures for millennia. And yet I could not help feeling that nature was being commodified again. The dominant narrative when it came to blue health still emphasized what water can do for us – nature *for* us, rather than us as part of nature.

In many studies on the therapeutic benefits of blue space activities such as surf or sailing therapy, the inclusion of the characteristics of water, as living or animate with its own life force, was largely absent. Often there was little or no description of the water, its particular qualities and the study participants' relationship with the water, or acknowledgement of human relationships with other-than-human beings and ecosystems. Unsurprisingly, with a few notable exceptions, most of these studies were carried out in western societies.

It became apparent to me that our health is tied to the health of water, and that it is impossible to restore our health without first restoring our relationship with water. The water in our bodies mirrors the water around us – when we wash, cook and drink. Water helps us to experience the interrelatedness of all life. It affects and is affected by everything it comes into contact with, bringing and transmitting information, physical and vibrational, from every encounter it has along the way. I address this key concept within this book.

Changing relationships

Our human relationship with water is in crisis. This is deeply political, and how we understand healing and health has been drastically colonized. There is a belief that we can "control" or "manage" water – that water is made somewhere by someone who bottles and sells it, that toxic microplastics flow in our rivers, ocean and bloodstream, or that in order to make water "safe" it must be sterilized. To capture the full complexity of the water crises and conflicts would be well beyond the limits of this book. However, I do seek to explore how we (the dominant, so-called modern society many of us live in today) might renew our understanding of the power and changing patterns of water in our lives.

The human quest to seek the healing benefits of water will fail if we approach water as another resource or commodity. "Whatever we do to water reflects back on us," wrote environmental journalist Charlie Ryrie in her book *The Healing Energies of Water*, "and whatever we do to our bodies also reflects back on us."[4]

Botanist and member of the Potawatomi Nation, Robin Wall Kimmerer calls this renewal of relationship with the living world reciprocal restoration. She argues that the restoration of our relationships with land and water is as essential as cleaning up pollution or proper hydrology. Without a more intimate reconnection of people and waterscapes, any restoration work is futile.

We live in a time when the fictional concept of rigid impenetrable lines or borders between nations, species, communities, weather systems, ecologies and climates is shifting and dissolving. The growing tensions between inequality, poverty, water and health, and the urgency of the fight to restore and protect our waters, actually demands that we slow down. As Nigerian philosopher and activist Bayo Akomolafe has explained, slowing down is the invitation to see in new ways. Waterscapes offer us these liminal places of surrender, where, in Bayo's words, "the sacred presses so close on the membrane of the ordinary"[5] that it can be felt. Bayo urges us not to jump into fixing problems or finding solutions without first slowing down so that we can be alive to beauty. Those cracks where the water spills out offer other ways of being in the world. Our contact with, and immersion in, water has this powerful ability to alter our perspective, perception and introduce us to a more sensuous way of knowing. That is what I hope you will begin to feel as you read this book.

A constantly changing cycle

To change our relationship with water, we first need to understand it and how the water cycle is interwoven into and through all life. We need water for our survival, and the water we have today is the same water that has always been here for billions of years. It allows life to exist on this blue planet, yet scientists can't fully fathom where water came from or how it formed. Some theories suggest that the water on Earth came from icy, mineral-rich comets that, billions of years ago, crashed into Earth and melted. It must have been an almighty asteroid storm that smashed into the planet to deliver the amount of water in our oceans.

Water is also known as H_2O, which means it is composed of two hydrogen atoms and an oxygen atom. Our solar system and the universe are awash with the chemical elements that create water. Hydrogen atoms were released during the Big Bang that kickstarted this universe, while oxygen atoms were formed in stars. When hydrogen and oxygen make a strong bond, drawn together by shared electrons, this releases energy that creates water. However, it is very difficult to find the right stable climatic state that allows water to take its liquid form. Most of the water discovered in our solar system is found in frozen seas of ice or giant clouds of vapour.

The water that moves through the plant life that covers Earth's surface is almost the same volume as the amount of water carried to the ocean in all the rivers of the world.[6] Water is a shapeshifter as it cycles through the Earth's systems and changing climate, becoming vapour, solid, liquid or gas. It can transform into mist, cloud, rain, snow, glacier, aquifer, lake, dew, spring, creek, rivers over land, delta, estuary, ocean, rivers underground, and even rivers in the sky. Scientists call this constant process of change the hydrologic or water cycle.

Water covers 71 per cent of the surface of the Earth, yet most of it is not accessible, or it is too salty or too polluted for us to use. This leaves 1 per cent of all the world's freshwater available for daily human use, or about 0.003 per cent of all water on Earth.[7] The types of freshwater we have access to come from different sources – from the groundwater of aquifers and wells, the surface water of rivers and lakes, and glacial meltwater. Water in all these forms is fast becoming scarce, polluted or overextracted.

Water's sacred connection

Our knowledge about the science of water still does not tell us very much about what water actually *is*. Perhaps this is because we are asking the wrong questions.

Lawyer and water protector Kelsey Leonard asked the audience during her TED talk to "Imagine if we asked *who is water?*"[8] Asking "Who is water?" in the same way we might ask someone who their grandmother or sister is, fundamentally transforms how we think about water, she explained. This creates a relational connection with water, changing the way we make decisions about how we engage with it, and how we might protect it, in the same way we would protect our grandmothers, mothers and sisters.

Water is a conduit and communicator of vital information. "It is everywhere and in everything," wrote Charlie Ryrie in *The Healing Energies of Water*.[9] Water's stable, three-dimensional structure allows it to vibrate at different frequencies. These vibrations inform all of life's processes, as water is "constantly receiving and transmitting energy from or to all it comes into contact with".

Water, according to Theodor Schwenk, a German teacher and follower of Steiner, is also nature's sense organ.[10] And Ryrie believed that water is not a self-contained substance but is always interacting with other molecules. The situation or environment that water finds itself in will alter its structure, leaving an imprint of where it has been and all that it has experienced. "If you put water from a jug into the cupped hands of two different people, you instantly obtain three different kinds of water," Ryrie wrote.

Water changes everything it touches. It is a solvent, dissolving and freeing elements from one state into another. The water held in our hands is affected by the chemical information contained on our skin, and even by our very pulse, explained Ryrie. This also means that water is affected by the environment it moves through. Underground water is affected by power cables and exposure to other electromagnetic fields that can destroy water's molecular structure. If water moves through a polluted environment, it picks up these pollutants, which can block its ability to communicate.

The same goes for the water in our bodies, with every cell needing water to communicate to be healthy, and the human body consists of 60 to 70 per cent water. Ryrie explained how our exposure to the environment we live in imprints new vibrational information onto us. If the water we drink is unhealthy, our body becomes unhealthy too. Our connection is so intertwined that plastic particles invisible to the naked eye are present in most of the world's drinking water and are now entering our bloodstream and mother's breastmilk.

In 1988, in a paper published in the scientific journal *Nature*,[11] French immunologist Jacques Benveniste and colleagues identified water's ability to give and receive information. His study found that water molecules seemed somehow to retain the memory of antibodies they had come into contact with, even when these antibodies were no longer present in the diluted solution. Later, because his study couldn't be replicated following conventional scientific method, his findings were dismissed as "fringe science" by his peers. Yet no one could explain how such a "memory" effect was discovered at all.

This revelation of the "memory of water" is something that was already known by Indigenous people and ancient wisdom traditions all over the world. It plays a prominent role in various mythologies across cultures. In ancient China, water from glaciers was considered the most vital and pure and was stored in jade vases. The Incas and Aztecs put water in jars of obsidian. The minerals from these containers, such as silica, were known to help water maintain its structure (or purity) and prevent it from becoming stagnant or polluted.

Conventional (western) science still largely fails to acknowledge the existence and value of older science from Indigenous cultures. However, science today has begun to reaffirm what Indigenous cultures have always asserted – that the soil and the trees are alive, and so is water, the giver of all life. This completely alters our relationship and interaction with water, restoring a more intimate and sacred connection.

Although scientists can't agree on the origins of water and how it came to be here on this planet, Indigenous science has always known and taught that water is spirit, the source of all life. The story of our human life begins in water. Restoring our sacred relationship with water through ritual and restoration is essential if we are to heal the waters of the world and, because we are water, heal ourselves. As we learn to be more like water, we become more fluid in our responses and less reactive, no longer resisting but able to flow.

My own water heritage

Water fills me with wonder. I feel woven by threads of water, myth and ancestry, and I feel the hum of saltwater in my veins. I was born in Ireland, an island nation in the North East Atlantic where rock and sea collide in Donegal Bay. This is a place where even though water was holy, the sea remained a place of loss and leave-takings for centuries. I am named after a wave at a river mouth that is, in turn, named after the salmon that run the river. My birth place and home is in the catchment of Durnesh Lough, a unique coastal lagoon and wetland and designated a Special Area of Conservation.

This book is a reflection of the waters I have come to know. It is deeply enriched by the words and water wisdom of many others, who are all, in their own way, keepers, protectors, healers and bearers of water. In the words of water protector Darlene Sanderson from Cree

Nation, this story attempts to follow "the veins and arteries of Mother Earth". Sanderson says that "water, like spirituality, needs to be experienced to be described".[12]

Perhaps this book will become a time capsule of how our relationship with water once was. Perhaps it will be part of an era that heralds a powerful reawakening of water cultures, river guardians, water protectors and marine citizens, of the restoration and healing of water and our own health. Or perhaps it will be an epitaph for how water once was, for all that we have lost and can never recover.

When writing this book, I was pregnant with twins. I never realized how much my relationship with water would change when I became pregnant, and how much more water my body needed to create more blood, to grow bone, to transport nourishment to my womb, the amniotic fluid expanding my belly, the water protecting new life growing within me from external shocks. I was so used to being master and commander of my body, shaping and honing, training it to ride fearsome waves, hold my breath, swim and paddle for hours on end in cold water.

My body is my ocean-going vessel, but during my pregnancy I lost that. When I went into the sea, I felt sea sick for the first time in my life if the water was too rough or choppy. I could no longer trust my breath or my lungs when held under a wave as my cardiovascular system worked in overdrive, circulating over twice as much blood to support new life growing inside me.

During pregnancy, I discovered the profound benefits of cold water immersion. This carries some risks – sudden immersion without first acclimatizing the body can trigger a "cold water shock response", causing the heart rate to go up at first. However, I greatly minimized any risks with a gentle and gradual buildup of regular immersion, combined with deeper, slower breaths and growing familiarity and understanding of both my body and the body of water I was entering. In the early months surfing, I experienced the joy of the glide, held by the water, weightless, just as my babies were held within me. Later, when swimming, I marvelled at the sensation of lightness and the connection with new life growing in my watery womb. A recent medical study suggests that regular cold water immersion could lead to a reduction in difficulties during labour and negative birth outcomes.[13] This is likely caused by the "low dose" of novelty and challenge being immersed in the sea creates, leading to an adaptive response and enhanced resilience.

I can't help imagine how the world might be for our children and all the generations to come. It will no doubt be a future shaped by the fate of water and will likely be more oceanic – rising seas reclaiming the land, ruined cities submerged underwater giving rise to new Atlantean legends, and perhaps new cities built floating above the waters. Water as we know it will be gone.

Becoming a mother reinforced for me the need to dig deep, to offer blood, sweat and tears to encourage the restoration of water and to honour and celebrate its rare and precious lifegiving force. With the warming of the rivers and seas and the melting of the ice, and rains that fail to return, it is all the more important to recover and retell the lost words, stories, knowledge and wisdom of water from our elders, ancestors and its protectors. In part, this book is an act of remembrance, so that some day humanity may recover some of the fragments of what once was and mourn what may never be.

What to expect in this book

To write about water is to write about the story of the world – of life itself. This book draws on my personal experiences and direct encounters of aliveness with water in its many different forms and at various times in my life. When reflecting on the meaning of these encounters, I weave insights from mentors, guides and teachers – leading water protectors, healers, scientists, athletes, artists and activists – who offer a more holistic understanding of our relationship with water: water as sacred, water as life. This book is an invitation to learn from the perspectives of a diverse group of water protectors and waterkeepers, such as Native Hawaiian surfer-scientist Cliff Kapono, who combines both Indigenous and conventional science.

In the following chapters, I explore the unique characteristics and properties of water and how we may weave a more intimate relationship with water in all its forms in our lives. I ask you to consider the interdependence of your health and the health of water and to explore what a truly reciprocal relationship with water looks like. I also unravel how we might all begin to reconnect to the patterns and power of water, and the essential and sometimes unexpected role water plays in supporting the health and vitality of our bodies, minds, hearts and communities.

At the end of each chapter you will find new ideas and practical ways to engage with the patterns and power of water, for the benefit of your health and the health of the water. These practices are invitations to deepen our attention in different ways, engaging in active listening and intuitive and embodied ways of knowing, through stillness, movement and reflection. With the awakening of this reconnection with water, I hope it ignites within you a gratitude and motivation to care for and protect the waters that help us thrive.

Our connection with water in all its forms is central to our wellbeing. I have found that if we can deepen the meaningful ways in which we interact with water environments, or blue spaces, water can offer us a profound experience of healing, renewal and connection. Chapter 1 explores our human connection with water and the power and potential of water to restore a deeper connection to ourselves, each other and the natural world. At the end of the chapter is a reflective journaling exercise to help connect with your local water body and an embodied practice to help you tap into the health benefits of connecting with water.

Chapter 2 considers one of water's most potent qualities – its ability to flow. I unpack water as a powerful, living metaphor for flow and the benefits of inviting more flow into our lives. The chapter closes with an invitation to experience your own flow state through a movement practice.

Chapter 3 explores water as a living metaphor for how life ebbs and how embracing this transformative quality of water can help us be with powerful emotions and overcome unexpected moments of challenge and grief in our lives. The chapter ends by sharing the benefits of taking time to be still, to pause and simply be, by practicing a "sit spot" meditation by water.

Chapter 4 delves into the mystery of water – how it eludes our ability to fully "know" it, and how it is profoundly embedded in our myths, traditions, religions and spirituality, affecting our imagination and understanding of our place in the world. At the close of the chapter, you are invited to practise a deep listening exercise as a way to become more attuned to the mystery of water.

Chapter 5 is all about the incredible power of water as well as the impacts of our human attempts to control this power, and tracing some of the efforts of those who are rewilding water that has been tamed. The chapter ends by inviting you to consider your own relationship with water through a journaling exercise and a practice to create a reciprocal relationship with water.

Chapter 6 takes us to the edge of water's resilience and considers how deeply entwined climate change and the story of water are with our human health and wellbeing. In this chapter, as the water rises, we meet those who are rising up to protect and restore water. The chapter ends with an invitation to engage in collective action for water with two group exercises: story mapping and river walking.

Chapter 7 returns us to the heart of our connection with water and the tremendous restorative potential of water, if we learn to care for it. The final exercise at the end of the book is a guided visualization to connect with our hearts and the water flowing through us and all around us.

I encourage you to be creative and approach the offerings in this book with openness and curiosity. If you do not live near water, consider the more taken for granted places and moments when water shows up in your life – during a rainstorm, puddles in the street, in your shower or your cup of tea in the morning. As you engage with this book and the insights and practices in it, notice if your awareness and relationship with water changes. You may discover that by reconnecting with water in your everyday life, you begin to move more fluidly like water, able to trust the power of your own flow.

CHAPTER 1

CONNECTION

My ocean connection gives me balance and keeps me grounded. As a surfer and social ecologist, my life is lived by the tides and the cycle of the moon. From my home, I can hear the storms arriving from the Atlantic in the night, and I plan my day around tide charts and predicted swell heights. At times of wild uncertainty, the ocean, with the ebb and flow of its tides, is a place of constancy for me. It teaches me to be fully present with what is. This has come from years of the saltwater leaving its residue on my skin until I feel I too am part water.

Island connections

I felt a weight dropping off me the farther we moved away from the mainland and there was nothing but the open expanse of blue beyond me. My body softened and flexed, adjusting to the rise and fall of the choppy wind-swell running underneath the ferry as it chased down the capping white-horse waves. There was nowhere to be but here, now, beneath the long light of the summer solstice sun. The fresh smell of salt spray mingled with the sickly sweet scent of diesel fumes from the engine room and the faint hint of peppery tobacco from a deckhand smoking on his break. These were the heady smells of freedom as a small, jagged island began to rise steeply up out of the horizon.

I always seem drawn to islands in order to connect – Inis Oirr, Tory, Inishturk, Inishbofin, Newfoundland, San Juans, Galapagos, Lamu, Mentawai, Pohnpei, New Ireland, Fiji, Mamanunca, Samoa, Tahiti, Moorea, Tikehau, Hawaii, Cuba and Jamaica. Writer and doctor Gavin Francis also seeks out islands as a way to recalibrate his sense of what matters most. He wrote that islands offer a place of isolation where "the obligations and irritations of life would dissolve and a singular clarity of mind would descend".[1]

Ironically, rather than being places of isolation, islands historically held great importance as places of knowledge exchange, commerce and hubs for provisioning, especially when travel by land was much more dangerous and difficult, thick with dense forests and predatory animals. In a way, I seek that too, to be in active exchange with the island and its waters, provisioning my creative self with inspiration to write.

On my first afternoon on the island, I tucked myself into a shelf in the rocks out of the wind above the entrance to Portdoon, a naturally sheltered harbour protected from the open sea with a channel running through the rocks. In the 9th century Viking raiders used it to hide out and pirates used it over the centuries to attack passing boats. Today, only one local fisherman regularly fishes for lobster, mackerel and pollack in his *currach*, a small traditional boat just the right size to navigate the narrow entrance that is no more than 11ft (3½m) wide.

I often find it easier to think and follow my thoughts when I am next to water. The unique combination of water's soothing constancy allows my brain to relax, and sudden changes such as a breaking wave offer a stimulating sense of novelty and surprise. This combination triggers involuntary attention, a kind of effortless focus that activates my brain's default network. This part of the brain is associated with the capacity for spontaneous thought, problem solving and creativity.

The sea gently rose and fell just below my dangling feet as I read Emma Dabiri's illuminating and unflinching account of why race was created to create racist beliefs in the 17th century, in her book *What White People Can Do Next*.[2] Dabiri, an historian and scholar of African studies, argues that racism ultimately comes down to the illusion of dualism and false binaries created by capitalism spawned from the British colonial slave era of the 1660s. This has separated us not only from each other, but from the interconnectedness of all life.

Dabiri's words got me thinking about place and identity; in particular, the notion of marine citizenship or being a citizen of the sea. My identity feels deeply connected to the ocean and its health: how I feel a profound belonging and sense of home whenever I'm immersed in it, while at the same time being fully aware that I am also an interloper in this watery world, 95 per cent of which we humans have yet to fathom.

Ancestral aquatic connections

In Ihi Heke's *Atua Matua Māori Health Framework*,[3] water and the oceans are considered among our oldest ancestral connections, and therefore the most knowledgeable, alongside the celestial stars and Earth. These *atua*, environments or natural places, are considered to be learning institutes. When I first met Ihi on the northwest coast of Ireland at an event called First Nations Ireland some years ago, he told me that consciously or subconsciously we take on the positive attributes of a place we belong to. As someone who is from a coastal community and whose passion is tied to the ocean, that is the best place for me to begin my work, he said to me.

Heke affirmed this feeling I have always had of being shaped and formed by the Atlantic waters off Donegal Bay. He explained, for example, that those who come from a river environment may exhibit individual traits associated with the qualities of the river, such as a dynamic personality and the ability to persevere in the face of barriers by choosing other pathways. To successfully do anything in the ocean (surf, swim, fish), we must first acquire a deep relational knowledge of the nature of the *atua*, and this can only be achieved through repeated visits, observations and immersion in the water, throughout many seasonal, lunar and tidal cycles. The associated health benefits and physical activity are an incidental outcome of this experiential engagement with the attributes of the sea.

Connecting with the moment

The rising tide began to tug at my feet, the sharp coolness of the water contrasting with my sun-warmed flesh, causing a tingle to run through my body. Diving beneath the surface, duality dissolved. Holding a single deep inhalation of breath took me into another world, the only separation a thin surface layer of water between the world above and what lies below. Beneath the surface, everything changed. It became so much more animate and alive, full of movement and colour. The way the sunlight danced on the surface when I looked up from a forest of kelp, my body's natural buoyancy at this shallow depth pulling me toward the illuminated surface as I wove through the high tide cracks, crevasses and pools in the rocky coastline.

Thinking beneath the surface changes me. It helps me unhook from any gnawing niggles or worries as soon as I submerge my head. I feel unstuck. I am reminded of psychologist and author Elaine Kasket's description of Acceptance and Commitment Theory,[4] a model for developing greater psychological flexibility.

It strikes me that a similar process seems to kick in whenever I get in the water and feel that connection. There are three key elements to the model. The first is openness to experience, including diffusion – the ability to recognize many ways of seeing and being. Immersion in water is an embodied, multisensory experience, and the properties of water also allow us to literally see the world in a new way. Water scatters and diffuses light, creating unique patterns and changing colours.

The second element is awareness of the present moment, the observational self – the part of ourselves that is able to notice without judgement. The bodily experience of being in water creates a visceral sense of presence. Water also has an incredible capacity to trigger our involuntary attention, holding our awareness in that moment.

And finally, the third element is engagement. The willingness to act on our values, even, or especially, when the "demons" show up. Being immersed in water takes us out of our everyday landbased lives and beyond the zone of what, for many of us, feels most comfortable and familiar.

When immersing my face in water or diving beneath the surface and inhabiting the space between the inhale and exhale, any tension still held in my body causes discomfort and an immediate urge to resurface. But if I approach the space between my breaths with an openness and softness as I lower my face into the water, my entire body relaxes and feels like it is melting into the sea.

An additional element at play is curiosity, a willingness to be with or move into the unknown. Perhaps it is because I am out of my element, never able to be fully fish, and this is part of the allure.

Bonnie Tsui wrote in her book *Why We Swim* that time spent in water provides us with glimpses into another world, of what it is like to be a fish.[5] The freedom from earthly ties and the feeling of weightlessness can add to this otherworldly feeling, an altered state as if we are entering a lucid dream and are able to fly, arms outstretched, gliding, suspended, unaware even of the water, if just for a flash. This drifting allows the mind to wander, inviting in fresh and unexpected connections, and is why water enhances creativity. Tsui quotes American long-distance open-water swimmer Lynne Cox, who famously said, "Who needs psychedelics when you can just go for a swim in the ocean?"[6]

There is a surprising abundance of life in the waters off Portdoon, invisible from the dry rocks above. Holding my breath once more and ducking under, I spotted a large grouper, numerous wrasse and juvenile fish, all in one crack in the rocks. I hovered above the kelp forest, sea-trees swaying hypnotically to the gentle pulse of the nearshore swell and swirl of underwater currents. Tucking my knees under me, I swooped head first into the canopy of slippery, silky amber-coloured fronds tickling my bare arms and legs. I was one of eight million species, and everything was always in motion. Even the rocks were alive with encrusted barnacles, opening up their tiny mouths to feed on the incoming tide while rocky crevices sheltered lobster and eel.

Lulled by the magic of this pulsing underwater world, I hadn't noticed the cold. Hauling myself back out onto the rocks, my body shivered for a while until it absorbed enough sunshine and snacks to warm up again. Shivering is the body's way of trying to return to its regular temperature. It increases our metabolism, like a mini workout for the body, and one of the reasons why cold water immersion is believed to be good for boosting our immune system. Pat McCabe, Diné (Navajo) and Lakota ceremonial leader and activist actively committed to protecting the world's waters, described to me that breathtaking sensation when we enter cold water as being when the soul expands, or even jumps a little beyond the body for a moment before coming back in, bringing with it an incredible sensation of recalibration or reset.

Connecting with confidence

Early the next morning, the heavy rain and sea mist that rolled in from the Atlantic during the night had lifted, revealing once again the indented coastline and wavy outline of the Connemara mountain range across the water. The tide was in full flood, filling the small, sheltered bay of Portdoon, and the island's resident population of 50 tripled in size as families arrived on the ferry. All those who were either born on the island or are the descendants of those who lived there come back for a week every July for what is known locally as "Swim Week". It coincides with World Drowning Prevention Day – drowning is the world's third leading cause of unintentional-injury deaths.

We have a physical memory in our bodies of what it means to be home in water. When we are born into the world we all carry birth trauma, that separation from the sacred water that may only be healed by a return to that watery world. It is why water offers us what feels like an intimate invitation yet can also feel like a place of loss and forgetting. To connect with water properly, we need to feel confident when we are in and around it.

For generations in Ireland the sea was "taboo" for anything like recreation or play. Instead, it was a place of risk, danger and violence, as well as an essential lifeline for sustenance, livelihoods and transport (or escape from poverty). Tragic drowning incidents are etched into plaques and memorials all along the coastline, especially the storm-battered west, instilling a legacy of fear – that it was better not to go near the sea at all rather than try to learn to swim. Today, the benefits of water confidence and knowing how to swim are well known.

The water temperature hovered around 14°C (57°F). Girls in their mid teens were leaping off the low pier. They were brimming with confidence and moved with ease as they pulled each other back and forth across the water using various rescue techniques demonstrated on land by their swim instructor.

A recent global study by Gallup found that there are enormous gender gaps in the ability to access water for recreational benefit, and the majority of us, worldwide, can't swim.[7] Most of these are women, with two in three women unable to swim unassisted. Implementing programmes that teach people – particularly women and girls – how to swim from a young age is an important way to equip them with a necessary skill that could save lives, especially in island and coastal communities.

By the afternoon the sun had unexpectedly burned through the cloud cover. The swim instructor surrounded by over 20 children selected a handful at a time. They waded into the shallows clutching brightly coloured soft foam floats and formed a small circle, lying on their bellies and holding their heads just above the water. They were instructed to take a breath in and lower their faces. Tentatively at first, they did as they were asked.

This was the first time they had put their faces into the sea, unknowingly triggering a cascade of remarkable biological and physiological responses, including the mammalian dive reflex, which linked them to their aquatic ancestors in the primordial ocean. Our bodies are designed to respond to the touch of water through thermoreceptors on our skin, which are connected to nerve endings that fire signals from our body to our brain, attuning us to our environment and to the water.

As the girls blew bubbles on their outbreath and practised controlled breathing, their bodies began to relax a little more, their arms spread out like starfish. Being immersed in cold water for as little as one minute increases electrical impulses in our brain. In turn, the firing of these neutrons is enabled by the connective molecular structure of water. Nerve receptors in our face respond to the sensation of water to help prepare our body to hold our breath so that we can dive.

The girls' little heads jerked back once all the bubbles had been exhaled, gasping with delight, their feet dancing on the sand. They were learning to bring an awareness of the sea into their bodies by focusing on the feeling of each breath in water and how their body responds. This connection between body–mind–place can help turn a potentially fearful experience into an enabling one.

African-American marine biologist and author Dr Ayana Elizabeth Johnson says that learning to swim changed her life. Johnson wrote on her Instagram page @ayanaeliza in July 2021 that this was not only because it inspired her to become a marine biologist but because she has always felt comfortable and happy in the water. Johnson explained how the terrible legacy of racism in the United States, with black people being excluded from pools and beaches, has left black children without opportunities to learn to swim, and with the highest rate of drowning. Johnson, whose parents taught her to swim, shared that if a parent does not know how to swim, there is only a 13 per cent chance that their child will learn.

To break that cycle, Johnson teamed up with the YMCA to offer the "Safety Around the Water Program" to children for free or at minimal cost so they could learn essential water safety skills. "Just think," Johnson wrote, "how much more diverse the field of marine science would be if more kids had the chance to learn to swim – and how much more we would know about the ocean if a broader diversity of people were designing marine research. And how much more 'effective' ocean conservation would be if the experts were as diverse as the coastal communities where they work, let alone as diverse as marine ecosystems." Opening a world of possibilities to safely fuel their curiosity all starts with learning to swim. "The self-discovery and the self-awe of learning to swim," she adds, "are the purest of delights. That feeling of confidence that comes from competence . . . I wish that for every child."

Connecting through play

New experiences and encounters of aliveness can deepen our connection with water. Play is one of the key ways in which we regulate our nervous system, activating our vagus nerve through reciprocal interactions and movement. The vagus nerve travels from the brain stem into our chest, heart, lungs and abdomen. Its front branch regulates the part of our parasympathetic nervous system associated with a state of rest and digestion. It helps to downregulate our nervous system after our survival mode has been activated by the sympathetic nervous system – the "freeze, fight or flight" response to a threat. In essence, activating the vagus nerve helps our body recalibrate after it has experienced stress, bringing it back into balance and a state of calm.

Neuroscientist Stephen Porges, author of *The Polyvagal Theory* and a leading advocate for activating the vagus nerve as a way to allow greater healing, suggests play is one of the key ways we can do this.[8] Play is what our nervous system needs to explore this planet and to feel calm and whole. In the water, the psychological benefits are enhanced even more, deepening our patterns of connection through visceral encounters of aliveness with the movement of waves, the texture of shifting sand and encounters with other species. It also helps us to build trust again – in our bodies, in each other and in the sea. We will explore this in more depth in Chapter 4.

Seeking rest and restoration

During the pandemic, connecting with the sea was a source of constancy for me. I have never been more grateful for its ability to soothe, hold, listen and restore, and for the privilege of having the wild North Atlantic Ocean on my doorstep. And I am not the only one.

Until recently, the desire for year-round immersion in the frigid waters off Ireland (where water temperatures are 8–10°C (46.4–50°F) for most of the year) was mainly considered to be the reserve of a few *mad eejits*. However, the pandemic has seen a huge surge in the numbers of people going to the coast or inland lakes and waterways to be in water, and the number of people participating in ocean- related watersports has more than doubled in the UK.

Open-water or "wild" swimming in particular has become so popular that every outdoor clothing store or surf shop ran out of *robies* in the summer and winter of 2020; these towel-like waterproof ponchos have become *de rigueur* for cold water swimming. A study by Surfers Against Sewage in 2020 estimated that the physical and mental health benefits from this increased engagement in ocean- and water-related activities could save UK National Health Services up to £20.2 billion annually.⁹ The pan-European Blue Health research study concluded that water environments are the most psychologically restorative of all environments.

This is not a recent phenomenon. The manipulation of water for aesthetic and restorative purposes was a central part of the culture during the Moorish reign of Spain. Water formed the focal point in architecture, including elaborate fountains to encourage calm and reflection and bath houses as a form of hydrotherapy, similar in design to those used by the ancient Romans. In the British Victorian era, the "new wonder drug prescribed for the nasty health effects of urban living"[10] was cold seawater, giving rise to the seaside resort. In Ireland, a history of harvesting seaweed for various therapies, including seaweed baths, dates back to at least the 12th century.

Caitriona Lynch, founder of Ebb and Flow Aquatics, a swim programme that introduces adults to sea swimming in Galway Bay on the west coast of Ireland, told me she had never seen so many people in the sea as she did during the summer of 2020. "It was powerful," she said. "People really needed the sea. They were desperate for it. People who always do it needed it; people who never did it before needed it. They needed the sea, the water and that sense of community, doing something together, and it gave them so much."

Perhaps by swimming in the sea we are seeking the experience of being alive. The ability to enter the water transports us to another world, helping us shed our land-based personas or baggage and embrace a beginner's mindset, deepening our connection in the most powerful, full-bodied and liberating way. Sea swimmer and author Tamsin Calidas writes about how standing naked at the water's edge ignites a brave new consciousness, recalibrating her inner compass.[11]

For Josephine Mandamin, Anishinaabe elder and water-rights advocate, there are times when standing by the water she can feel the pulsing of the water on the shore. "I can feel that connection myself with the water," she says.[12]

Bonnie Tsui has also come to appreciate the aliveness of water, and through swimming has discovered an intimacy with watery places in a way she never imagined possible.

Despite the pleasures and joys associated with engagement with water, the lack of support or initiatives educating such a huge influx of people new to the sea and open water can become a problem. It takes time and careful observations to learn how to read the water or how to be in the open water safely, and Caitriona noticed there were a lot of risky behaviours and incidents happening at her local swim spot in Galway.

"It's really important to educate people," Caitriona said. "It's not just about your personal experience, it's about the environment you're in; knowing the tides, winds and geography of a place." Her open water swimming programmes take a mindful approach, teaching people how to read the conditions, the tides, the rise and fall of the waves, the energy of the wind, and how all these elements interact with the inner ebb and flow of our own emotions. "For me, what's really important," she adds, "is helping people appreciate that it's bigger than them and their experience. You're part of this amazing place and protect it and mind it for yourself and other people."

Blue care

Perhaps unsurprisingly for those of us drawn to the sea, the unique qualities of water have a positive effect on the human body – tapping into these healing qualities is called "blue care". Evidence shows how blue spaces, outdoor bodies of water, are associated with a lower risk of depression, anxiety and other mental health disorders, as well as greater relaxation in adults and improved behavioural development and social connection in children.

Research measuring human brain waves suggests that water has a calming effect on the mind. Over 30 years ago, behavioural psychologist Roger Ulrich carried out EEG tests to measure how different natural environments may alter the rhythmic patterns of alpha waves in the brain.[13] Increased alpha waves are linked with relaxed mental states, while decreased alpha waves are associated with improved focus and attention. While rigged up to machines, participants in the study viewed a series of images of different types of environments: natural, rural, urban and manmade. During water scenes, alpha waves were *higher* on average than during urban scenes. Water scenes also had a more positive influence on emotional states than any of the other types of environments. More recent evidence also supports that "exposure" to water aids a quicker recovery from a stressful event.[14]

Studies have found that water sounds have the greatest positive effect on our health than any other sounds, helping us to control our mental states, reduce stress and restore our attention.[15] In a world filled with the constant noise of industrial, urbanized, "modern" living, blocking out natural sounds and provoking constant vigilance, the value of water sounds can't be underestimated. It is thought that the calming benefits of water sounds may relate to the critical role of water for survival, as well as the capacity of water to mask noise. Perhaps the benefits are also linked to how sounds were carried to us through water while we were carried in the womb, and to our ancestral connection with water as the source of life.

Being active in water can benefit our physical and mental health and improves the flow of blood in our bodies much more than other activities such as cycling or running. In people who immerse their bodies regularly in water, the pressure of the water can help to lower their blood pressure over time by pushing blood from their extremities to their heart and lungs. When moving our bodies through water, we meet a certain resistance. This helps to build up strength in our muscles and joints without any wear and tear. The low impact of swimming helps to reduce pain so it is possible to do it late into your life.[16]

An understanding of water's unique healing properties could have tremendous benefits for human health. The mist and spray released by breaking waves and waterfalls is believed to contain aerosols and negative ions that may help reduce breathing difficulties by reducing inflammation. The benefits of improved lung function can last several months following visits to powerful waterfalls.[17]

Another common factor to emerge from studies into blue care, in particular swimming and surfing, is the joy people experience from doing it. In an outdoor survey in Ireland carried out during the first Covid-19 lockdowns of 2020, respondents said the primary motivation for going swimming was not to keep fit or to be physically active but was for how good it made them feel. Similarly in the UK, people's primary motivation for spending time by the sea was to relax and unwind. People intuitively go to water to self-regulate their emotional states. Open water swimmer Karen Throsby wrote about the unexpected sensory pleasures of marathon swimming and that if she goes into the water "like a cranky sea lion", she always comes out "like a smiling dolphin".[18]

Reconnecting with ourselves

A sense of belonging does not always have to come from social connection with other humans. For some regular watergoers, we need to be alone so that we can reconnect with ourselves. For Caitriona Lynch, swimming alone offered a reprieve. "Me, alone with the sea. It felt like this is actually my home, right here," she told me.

Water has the capacity to facilitate a full bodied sense of connectedness with life. At a time when loneliness is skyrocketing and poses a threat to our mental health, connections or attachments to places, especially natural environments, may help to buffer the psychological effects of loneliness. This seems to be even more enhanced when we are in blue spaces.

A recent national study on nature connection for health and wellbeing in Ireland found sea swimming to be one of the most effective outdoor activities for significantly enhancing a sense of connectedness.[19] This may be linked to it being a highly immersive and stimulating activity – taking in all the movement, colour, sounds, sensations and textures through all of the senses. One woman in the study explained how the sea kept her together when she felt like her world was falling apart.

Many people who swim will attest to a feeling of freedom, not only from bodily constraints while being held by water, but also from being immersed in an environment free of judgement. With the body submerged and supported, there is no need to feel lumbering or aged, or to be restricted by the confines of a broken body. Research by cardiologist and longevity researcher Hirofumi Tanaka confirms that weightlessness is one of the key factors that makes swimming so good for the body, especially if it is ageing or injured.[20] In the water, bodies are free from any pain caused by the impact of land-based activities. In cool or cold water the benefits are enhanced by reducing inflammation.

For people with sensory impairment, water's multisensory nature offers a powerful way to reconnect with the world. Health geographer Dr Sarah Bell, who is based at the University of Exeter, spent a number of years with people living with visual impairment to understand their experiences of nature as part of the *Sensing Nature* project.[21] She talked to me about some of the women she met and their relationships with water. Their names have been changed to honour their anonymity.

Megan, in her thirties, lost all sight in an accident some years ago and is a wheelchair user at times, depending on her energy levels and joint pain. She described the experience of being submerged in water as "a really nice feeling of total weightlessness". The feeling of being suspended beyond her depth and not able to touch the bottom eased the pain in her damaged legs and feet.

Viv, in her forties, with a congenital condition causing retinal detachment, reflected on her experiences when swimming and the importance of the elevated feeling of touch when in the sea. "To have this feeling like it's sort of embracing you. . . it was fabulous," she said.

Amelia, in her fifties and partially sighted, described how empowering it felt to sail. Sailing, she explained, isn't necessarily to do with what you can see but "quite a lot of it's what you can hear, and what you can feel". Being immersed and exposed to the water, wind, weather and skies helped to build her confidence too.

In recent years, parasurfing (or adapted surfing) has been growing rapidly. I spoke with three times world parasurfing champion and Britain's only world surfing champion Melissa Reid about how being in the sea offers her a sense of belonging. Reid is also a Paralympic bronze medallist in triathlon and is partially blind with no peripheral vision. Having surfed since the age of eight, she tells me she feels more at home on water than on land – "There is no judgement."

For Reid, it is an entirely embodied experience. "I go on feel; feeling the wave pull back. I have no depth perception so I sense the speed to know when to do a bottom turn. Or I sense how the board feels under my feet."

Having a network of support from her coaches and other surfers really helps. Her coach uses goggles to replicate Reid's extremely limited vision in the surf so he can better communicate with her and understand how it feels in the body to turn the board when she can't see the wave at all. Similarly, in Australia, surfer Matt Formston, who is 95 per cent blind, described in a 2021 interview with the *Sydney Morning Herald*[22] how he feels the water through his body, such as the vibrations of the water in his stomach through the board. His hearing is heightened and he can read the ocean by listening to it. The movement of the sea, the warmth of the sun and the steadfast wind direction all help him pinpoint his position. For both Reid and Formston, it is clear that water is their solace, that it is the place that is always accepting of who they are.

Our inner need for water

In many Indigenous teachings, water is acknowledged as the first foundation of life. Mona Polacca, a member of the *Havasupai* or "People of the Blue Water" tribe in Arizona, USA, wrote that we were birthed from our mother's womb and we followed the water into this world.[23] Some 375 million years ago our arms, legs, necks and lungs were bequeathed to us by a fish that crawled out of the primordial sea onto land.[24]

Water plays an essential role in every function in our body. We are waterbound. And as with all waterbound creatures who spend too long out of the water, wrote Iranian physician Dr Batmanghelidj (also known as "Dr Batman"), we too become severely stressed when we fail to respond to our body's need for water.[25] When our body becomes dehydrated – the loss of water in its cells – it becomes stressed and even more dehydrated, creating a vicious stress response cycle. Simply put, the loss of water in the body is a precursor for many disease conditions.

Our body is comprised primarily of fluid, and water is constantly cycling through us. Just as there is a complex weave of waterways crisscrossing the planet, there are waterways within our body. Dr Batman describes how these waterways and circulatory channels transport information, hormones and other "products" (even memories) that are created in our brain to nerve endings throughout our body to use in the transmission of messages. We, too, are part of the water cycle.

Although western medicine is still criticized for dismissing the vital role of water in curative and preventive treatments in favour of various pharmaceutical medicines, the notion of water as a conduit is predominant across Indigenous teachings. In Mohawk, a language spoken by a few thousand Native Americans, water is called *ohnekanos*, meaning spirit, the spirit that brought all life here. If understood in this way, water means how we came to be here spiritually.

According to Mohawk elder Jan Longboat's teachings,[26] water is a conduit for all of who we are – not just our genetic material but our feelings, our spirit. This is carried in the water inside the womb and released with us when we make the transition to the physical world. In a paper documenting the reflections from 11 First Nations, Inuit and Métis Grandmothers, titled *Aboriginal Women, Water and Health*, Longboat explained that this process signifies a commitment between the spirit world and the physical world, emphasizing, "We made a pact that we would never leave each other, and so that water will always take care of us."

Water is more than a metaphor. In the roar of the sea I can roar my own feelings, releasing the feeling held too tightly in between my tense shoulder blades or knotted stomach. I can cry freely too, my salty tears indistinguishable from the rest of the saltwater. It also gives me permission to feel joy. The simple joy of being, in every cell of my body.

More-than-human connections

When we are by a body of water as vast as the ocean, we can sense that we are in the presence of something so much greater than ourselves, as if connecting to a higher power. There are often greater opportunities for interactions with other species at coastal and waterside locations, such as birds, fish, otters, seals and other marine mammals, and even crabs scuttling across the sand, all enhancing a sense of interspecies connection.

As mentioned in this book's introduction, the water we use and bathe in today is the same water that has been on Earth for billions of years "You'll never know everything that the water is," water protector Pat McCabe, also known as "Woman Stands Shining", told me. "Science calls it H_2O. That barely even touches it."

McCabe shared with me the scientific version of the water cycle she was taught in school: how water travels in a continuous loop, evaporating from the ocean into the air to form the clouds before becoming rain and falling back down to the land through the rivers, and finally returning to the ocean.

"But they leave out the fact that every being, every living thing, is drinking that water first," she said. "So it's actually being filtered through the body, and that's just the surface layer. It's also being filtered through the consciousness of all life."

I asked her to explain what she meant by the "consciousness of all life".

In teachings from her elders, McCabe was told that water is also being filtered through time because the water that exists now has always been present. She asked me to imagine how all of our ancestors drank from the same water. "Not only our ancestors," she added, "but all of the birds and the fish and all the beetles and butterflies, deer, elephants, everybody, and all of their ancestors." To illustrate, McCabe held up a small clear glass of water and said, "Tyrannosaurus Rex had a drink of this!"

As McCabe explained, water connects us with the lineage of all life. "No wonder water can change the way our minds are working and our hearts are working." She said this is especially the case when we evoke and invoke water in ceremony.

This resonates with Hawaiian surfer and biochemist Dr Cliff Kapono's "Surfer Biome" project investigating interspecies connections between humans and the more-than-human world we are immersed in, especially in the world of water. Combining conventional Western and Indigenous sciences, Kapono, who lives in Hilo on the Big Island of Hawaii, revealed that we share the same water bacteria on our skin and in our microbiome as when we regularly immerse ourselves in the sea as whales.

Kapono's ancestors sailed across the deep ocean from Tahiti some 90 generations ago. When they arrived in Hawaii, his family became known as the "protectors of the sacred", and "the astonishing waters" was another name given to his family to honour where they came from. Kapono carries his family lineage and naming well. He uses surfing as a novel way to elevate conversations around ocean health. He has shaped himself into a "surfer-scientist". Kapono explained how this elevated his social standing, voice and visibility as a minority through his education. "It was a way for me, on a personal level, to prove to society that there exists a place for someone who is proficient in the ocean and in science," he said. "I wanted to show that I didn't have to choose, to bring surfing and science together."

Kapono supports the idea that we are nature. "When we get out of the water," he explained to me, "the ocean leaves its fingerprint on us. Different seas, different waters, leave different fingerprints. Likewise, we, too, leave our fingerprints wherever we go, in more ways than one."

Remarkably, only one per cent of the genetic material in our microbiome is actually human. The other 99 per cent comes from somewhere else, from other bacteria in the environment around us. Kapono wanted to provide empirical evidence that we are natural beings, completely interconnected and interdependent with the living world around us. He told me he was able to discover that there are certain microbes that colonize the human skin that distinguish surfers from non-surfers.

His research reaffirmed the Indigenous story of his people. He said: "It became a way to celebrate my Indigenous understanding that we are nature and use conventional science to show that there are these signatures, we just never thought about it that way before. The separate worlds we think about are actually connected by these molecular signatures."

Communicating with water

Kapono asked me to imagine how I choose to enter the water knowing that it senses me too. His and McCabe's words made me think about my own connection with water and how I encounter it and greet it, if at all. How do I first introduce myself to a "new" wave? What is the appropriate greeting? How do I ask permission? Is this why my experience in the sea and surf differs greatly depending on how I enter it?

I thought about the times when I would pause in acknowledgement and appreciation of the water. When I would anoint myself with the saltwater, asking for the sea's blessing and protection, noticing its mood, textures and tones before plunging in. And also those times when I just charged in without a thought for the water – were those the times I got my ass handed to me, ending up dumped back on the shore after a wipeout? Not that the sea ever had a special vendetta against me in those moments; it wasn't "for me" at all. I had failed to enter the domain of water with pure intention, care and respect so I had not noticed or read the water properly. I did not hear what the sea was communicating.

Lakota skier Connor Ryan, who lives in Colorado, sings when he goes to the mountains to amplify his presence to let water in all its forms know that he sees it and he is willing to respect it. "Realizing that the place is experiencing you, as much as you are experiencing the place, is a really important attitude to cultivate," Ryan explained to me.

He introduces himself to the place, to the spirits of the water and the mountain, as a relative, another conscious being. "I try to sing traditional songs on my way out," he said. "I sing to the seven directions – the cardinal directions, the direction of Mother Earth and grandfather sky and finally the direction of my own heart. They're the principal directions the Lakota use to orient ourselves, both navigationally and spiritually and emotionally. I try to bring that to the forefront every day and just introduce myself."

This is what it means to cultivate a reciprocal relationship with water, and why it is so important from an environmental standpoint – to realize that our actions all the time impact the places we go to, the water we interact with and take joy from. "There's always some kind of exchange happening, all the time," Ryan said. "That really informs us to make decisions in a different way. And to know that she (Grandmother Earth) is perceiving these exchanges."

Singing in Lakota deepens this relationship. Like many Indigenous languages, Lakota is a language that does not see trees, mountains, rocks and water as inanimate objects or something that is not alive but speaks to everything relationally. "The trees are not the trees, they are *cha o yatey*, the nation of the trees," Ryan said. "Lakota recognizes the water's sovereignty and its right to exist." He adds that water remembers it was once spoken to much more nicely in Lakota than in English.

My conversation with Ryan reminded me of the songs of the shark callers of Papua New Guinea (PNG) and other parts of the South Pacific region, who sing the names of their ancestors and their respect to the sharks so that the sharks will come from the deeps and the hunt will be successful. It is a low-impact form of community fishing that honours the sharks' spirit and life force.

According to a report in *The Guardian* newspaper in 2021, the custom "is rooted in the belief that sharks carry the spirits of ancestors and that by adhering to strict protocols, shark callers can beckon, capture and kill sharks without coming to harm".[27] In the same way that Connor Ryan's singing to the snow and mountain rivers honours the spirit and aliveness of place, the practice of shark calling acknowledges the reciprocal relationship between humans, sharks and the health of the marine ecosystem. When all these elements are aligned and the interconnection is recognized and acknowledged through song, there is balance in the system.

Godfrey Jordan Abage, an ocean activist and shark caller, said in *The Guardian* article that the practice creates a spiritual and cultural bond between the community and the health of the ocean. "You wake up by the shore, you listen to the waves, you can feel the waves, you get peace when you are under pressure, you sit under a tree and you get this cold breeze and you see the ocean – it is something that really connects our spirit," he explained.

Unfortunately harmful actions from outside forces severely threaten this balance in PNG. Activists such as Abage believe deep sea mining in PNG – one of the first places in the world where this has been approved – is having a disastrous effect on ocean health and disrupting interspecies communication and behaviour. Excessive runoff and flooding caused by illegal logging and deforestation on the islands is adding to the destruction of important coastal habitats, especially nursery grounds for fish, including sharks.

The loss of the practice of shark calling would mean the bond between communities and the more-than-human world of sharks would be broken. The knowledge of what a healthy community of sharks should be like would be gone, and the names of shark species forgotten. Abage said, "The shark can feel you and understand you, and so the communication between you and the shark is really about how you have lived your life."

Water is not there to heal us, according to Northern Irish writer Kerri ní Dochartaigh in her book *Thin Places*. "Nature is not somewhere we go into," she wrote. "Nature is not just 'my' river, or the tundra, the highlands, an island, an empty beach or a perfectly sculpted woodland. Nature is not always silent and a bringer of healing. It is not for any one type of person, with any particular background."[28]

Instead, how would the healing process be if we recognized water as alive? This is similar to the teachings of traditional plant healers and native herbalists – to always ask the plant's permission before taking it, and to always give thanks for all that it gives. I think this approach to water and to "blue health" would lead to a deeper, more reciprocal form of healing where first there is a process of initiation, to always ask permission, to always give thanks, rather than commodifying water as just another resource to serve our needs.

McCabe, Ihi, Ryan and the work of other water protectors all emphasize a need for a water-centred, rather than human-centred, approach to healing. One such approach is called "blue ecology",[29] a theory founded by Michael Blackstock of Gitxsan/European heritage and a senior negotiator with First Nations in British Columbia. This is a powerful reframing of the water cycle and is an ecological philosophy, which emerged from interweaving First Nations and Western thought that, as Blackstock explains, "acknowledges fresh and salt water's essential rhythmical life spirit and central functional role in generating, sustaining, receiving and ultimately unifying life". It places the importance on embracing a water-first approach when planning human interventions in the environment. You will read more about this in Chapter 5.

By consciously deepening our connection with water, we awaken the manifold benefits for the restoration of our wellbeing, such as recovery from stress and mental illness, greater relaxation and enhanced social connectedness. Immersion in water introduces us to a whole new sensory experience, helping to bring us back home to our bodies, our feeling, sensing selves. Our bodies are designed to respond to the touch of water. As Hanli Prinsloo, South African freediver and founder of I Am Water, explained to me, "When you're in the water you can't not be aware of your body."

This provides us with an incredible sensation of recalibration or reset. These connective properties of water extend beyond our minds and bodies. As McCabe explained, water connects us with the lineage of all life. Consciously or subconsciously we take on the positive attributes of a place we belong to. So much so, that the water bodies we are most attached to leave their fingerprints on us, altering our microbiome. Through this water connection we discover we are *fighte fuaighte*, to borrow the old Irish phrase, meaning woven into and through the living world around us, that we are water. A connection that is enhanced when we acknowledge and appreciate water's aliveness.

EXERCISE:
CONNECTING WITH WATER

Reflective practice:
How well do you know your water?

This exercise is about building relationships with water. As Dorothy Christian and Rita Wong wrote in *Downstream*, "when we go back far enough in our familial lines, we find ancestors who lived in relationship with lands and waters that they relied on for sustenance (. . .). This is a reminder that we wouldn't be here today if our ancestors had not had that relationship with water, living close to rivers, wells and sources of fresh water not only for sustenance and survival but for the sacred continuance of life."[30]

Take a journal or notebook and find a quiet moment, or a place to sit by your nearest body of water. Wherever you are, try to find a quiet space alone with yourself and journal (write, draw or record a voice memo) your response to the following questions:

1. Where is your water? Which water bodies are you connected to? (This may be a stream, river, lake, pond, canal, reservoir, well, spring, wetland, marsh, estuary or ocean.)
2. Where does your drinking water come from? Where is it sourced?
3. Where did your ancestors 100 years ago get their water?
4. What is the name of the river closest to your home?

5. Where is its source and ending?
6. Which other water bodies is it connected to?
7. For whom is this water home?
8. How is this body of water doing?
9. Which catchment or watershed do you live in? If you don't know, find out. For example, if you are in Europe, you can visit the European Atlas of the Sea and select your local catchment, or in the United States you can visit the US Geological Survey's map of watersheds and drainage basins.

Do not worry if you do not have immediate answers to these questions. Instead, use them as an opportunity to be curious and find out more about your local water.

Embodied practice: Connecting with your body and breath

The health benefits of floating in water are multifaceted and are especially impactful for those of us recovering from an injury, suffering joint or muscle pain or with mobility issues. Floating requires us to trust the water and its ability to hold us. To do that we have to relax our body, releasing any tension held there by bringing our awareness to our body through breathing. Floating aids muscle relaxation, helps to reduce chronic back pain and inflammation in the joints, lowers blood pressure and even improves sleep.

The next time you find yourself near a body of water, at a calm and safe spot to swim or immerse yourself, slowly enter the water and bring your focus to your breath. When you are about knee deep (or less), lower your body into the water and lie back – you can gently rest on your arms if you are not comfortable with floating, or use a float, especially if you are in freshwater where your body will be less buoyant than in saltwater. Spread your arms out from your sides and stretch your legs out as if you are a starfish. This will help your body balance.

Mentally scan your body from head to toe, noticing any tension. Wherever you feel tension, breathe into that part of your body. On your exhale, let your body soften, releasing the tension into the water. Inhale, then exhale.

As you inhale, notice how your lungs expand, like a balloon inflating, causing your body to feel a little lighter and float more easily on the surface.

Gently exhale and notice how your body begins to sink a little into the water.

With each breath, allow your body to soften, relax and be held by the water. Inhale, then exhale.

Now tuck your knees to your belly and roll over so you are no longer on your back but are kneeling in the shallow water. Using a float can help as you do this exercise.

To get used to putting your face into the water, take a deep, gentle breath in and lower your face to the surface of the water.

As your skin touches the water, begin to exhale, blowing bubbles with your breath. After you get used to the sensation of the water on your face, lower your face into the water a little more so that the water covers your ears.

Notice the difference in the sounds. Life below water has its own music, and everyday sounds appear different, travelling much faster underwater.

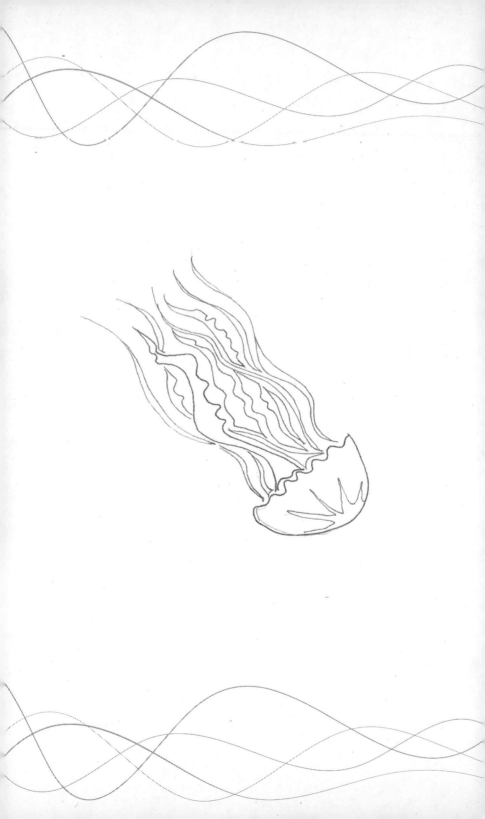

CHAPTER 2

FLOW

It is early and the light from the slowly rising November sun is a pale glow, barely seeping through the blanket of grey-blue cloud that seems to soften the still air. The tide has withdrawn, leaving behind a slick, shiny residue of saltwater, like a glossy glaze over the hard packed sand that mirrors the low slung sky perfectly.

The cold, wet sand stings my skin. Instinctively I try to pull my bare feet away, tiptoeing gingerly as if trying to avoid sharp, broken shards of glass. I remember to breathe, and as my body softens a little I slowly let my weight sink into my soles, the sand shifting beneath me. Soon the sensation of cold is gone. I can't tell if that is because my body temperature has adjusted or if my feet have begun to numb.

The 200,000 sensory receptors on the soles of each foot send mini, electrifying shock waves from the sand through my body to my brain, flowing along a complex and tangled network of nerve pathways. This provides feedback about my environment, helping my body to better "read" the shifting terrain, becoming more responsive to subtle changes. In traditional Chinese medicine, stimulating certain areas of the foot helps to release or balance energy flow in the body.

It is quiet on this westerly facing beach on the edge of the north Atlantic and I can't sense any rhythm or music that might help to guide my movement at first. I feel a little tense, so I close my eyes, breathe and listen for the sea. The constancy of the rhythmic pulse of the breaking waves has a soothing effect, flowing over my body like a sound bath, and the chatter in my mind dies down – the pulsing white noise hum of the surf fed by a light onshore breeze.

Our flow states

The concept of a flow state was popularized by psychologists Mihaly Csikszentmihalyi and Jeanne Nakamura,[1] to describe when you become fully immersed in whatever you are doing, so much so that you lose a sense of time, evoking pure joy or ecstasy. For this book, I wanted to better understand how people who are most immersed in watery environments experience flow, and whether a deeply intimate connection with water in all its forms (fluid, frozen, solid) could enhance this flow state.

I also wanted to understand if the fluid nature of water truly plays a role in shaping our own sense of fluidity of our mind, body and spirit. I learned that to be "in flow" is not only to be in a state of hyperfocus in the present moment. It is not just a sense of fluidity between the mind and body but also with the environment we are immersed in. To embrace our fluidity and find our flow requires an acknowledgement that we are about to enter into a relationship with the aliveness of the world.

On a beach on north Donegal, Māori physical activity and health expert Ihi Heke explained to me that flow can be understood as a "wairua-of-place", *wairua* being the spirit or life force. This can be experienced in those moments when we are most deeply immersed in our environment. Another understanding of *wairua* is a reflection, where the environment reflects who we are – our truth. As Ihi explained to me, we experience the spirit of a place when we are deeply connected to it and participate within it. My sea connection and relationship with the ocean comes from years of learning, struggling and practising. The *wairua* of sea might be revealed to me for a few fleeting seconds when I surf a wave, the wave expressing its spirit or essence through the body of the surfer.

The feeling of flow

It seems that flow can't be maintained as a constant state, and that ebb is necessary for flow. Iranian snowboarder and one of the pioneers of surfing in Iran Starma described flow as an oscillating wave. When not at her "peak performance", she is gathering her energy for the next phase. Flow is a release of energy but "the most amazing thing in life is the balance between these states," she told me. "It's important to not only focus on the peak."

Starma described the feeling of flow when she is snowboarding or surfing as the feeling of flying. "Feeling the power of nature that moves with you. The feeling of being close to God," she said.

Another athlete familiar with flow is professional skier, Connor Ryan from Lakota Nation, who explained that as a skier there is an inevitability of motion. "Flow definitely has this gravity to it," he said. "It's such a necessary part of what gives life to everything but in order to really be in flow there's this sense of letting go."

Connor described succumbing to gravity as he flies down a snow-covered mountain peak, and the lines he takes down a mountain as being his flow lines. Before committing to his line, there is an acknowledgement and appreciation that he is surrendering to something bigger than himself.

"I remember at the top of each one of those lines taking a moment to sing or pray in Lakota," he said.

"Recognizing we (skier, mountain, snow. . .) are all about to do something that's bigger than the experience, and then letting go. There's no forcing flow."

For Ryan, to be in flow is to participate with this collection of greater natural processes, entering into a stream of consciousness and energy. His training and preparation is about learning to recognize and embrace the conditions that allow that alignment to come together. "Be present within," he said, "and ultimately be grateful for it. Be in reciprocity with the flow. The more you learn how to embody that reciprocity, the easier it is to be in flow."

Flow and connection

It is impossible to be in the "here and now" if you are not connected to your body. Creating new experiences in our body that counteract old or habitual reactions that have been conditioned into us by our life experiences, history and even geography, allows us to reconnect to our intuitive self. The embodiment of the movement of other animals or the more-than-human world can help to free us from the aching bonds of earthly ties and help us be in a state of receptivity – allowing the sound of the waves or the wingbeats of the bird to flow through us.

On the beach that cold morning, I wanted to move, to find my flow. Tilting my head back, I looked skyward. A seabird – a fulmar, I think – crossed my vision, and I followed the invisible line it traced out toward the open water, its wings outstretched in an effortless glide before it banked into the wind. A moment of pause and then it dropped, swooping low, circling around its outstretched wing tip.

I moved my body gently and softly at first, as if I was testing my "wings", my spine slowly unfurling, shoulder blades sliding up and out, fingertips grazing the horizon line. I was not alone; I had a dance partner. Reflected on the sheen of wet sand was my mirror image – she was all fluid; she was water.

In the parts of our brain that sense feelings in our body, we have mirror nerve cells that fire whenever we observe the movements of others. This can lead to kinaesthetic empathy – feeling what it is like to be the person you are observing. This does not just apply to other humans; we can extend this capacity to mirror and experience empathy in this way to other animals, and even plants and natural phenomena such as the wind and ocean waves.

Kinaesthetic empathy recognizes our kinship with all living things. It helps to explain why I felt so compelled to move in the way I saw the seabird moving. Extending and bending my spine gently backward and unfurling my arms meant I was able to imagine what it feels like to be a fulmar, for a moment.

Ancestral movement expert Simon Thakur says we have an incredible ability to move our bodies in infinite and myriad ways so that we can mimic anything, even trees, water, rainfall and waves. He explains how this stems not only from our evolutionary biology as a means of survival but also from an ancient, prelanguage form of storytelling or "physical theatre" that helped our ancestors describe what we experienced in our environment through movement and mimicry.[2]

Awareness of our fluidity

The water cycle is not some abstract, neatly drawn graph with water moving in a tidy circular process going on somewhere in the background to our human lives. In actuality, it is messy, dynamic and entangled, with water replenishing, removing and cleansing our inner fluid systems. We are permeable and our skin is porous, with all the water in our body being replaced 17 times a year. We have something like 30 trillion cells in our body that all need water and movement to communicate with each other to be healthy.

As water protector Pat McCabe explained in Chapter 1, water is flowing and being filtered through the body of every being, every living thing, and through the consciousness of all life, across all time. Our bodies are connected to the watersheds and bodies of water that we live with and move through (see Chapter 6 for more about watersheds). All these waters have become part of us, continually cycling through us.

"To feel the sacredness of water, we humans must become fluid and feel our fluidity," wrote Canadian theologian and somatic psychotherapist Denise Nadeau in 2017. "If we are fluid, we are harder to control and less controlling."[3]

On the beach that November morning, as I moved I began to sense the water in my body and imagined how it would like to move. Becoming a breaking wave, swaying, rippling seaweed in a rush of tidal water, rising and falling with each breath, toes tracing circles on the sand – ankles, knees, pelvis, spine, ribs, shoulders, arms, neck, head and eyes all followed, spiralling like a moon shell. Moon shells found washed up on the tide line once belonged to sea snails. They are round, glossy and with a perfect spiral winding outward from the centre of the shell, the still point in the eye of a storm. My internal process began to shift, and I felt newly unearthed emotions surfacing from some hidden depth, a dance of contraction and expansion.

It is increasingly challenging to express "self" without censorship in the world today, especially for women or others in bodies that belong to a minority – black bodies,

bodies of colour, disabled bodies, non-binary bodies. Minna Salami, author of *Sensuous Knowledge*, wrote that being a woman in a patriarchal world means living a life of unmet desires.[4] As women, we are conditioned to move in the world in a certain way – to contract, withdraw, become small, maybe even invisible. This is a bodily response to staying safe. For some women, feeling unsafe and needing to contract can be an everyday reality, especially for bodies weighed down by centuries of oppression.

A more sensuous encounter with our body is one way we begin to expand after years of contraction. Encounters with water are one of the most sensuous experiences we can have – water affects our entire being, speaking to our body, mind and spirit. It is mentally stimulating, therapeutic, with the capacity to alter and transform our most ingrained thought patterns. There is also a certain all-enveloping intimacy to water; the way it can move over our bodies, touching every part of who we are, meeting a deeply human need for touch.

My experience of moving my body how it wanted to move that morning, being in direct contact with water on the wet sand, allowed me to internally begin to open up and face my discomforts in a playful way. In the same way I felt that seabird stretch out its full wingspan, I felt my body begin to expand a little too.

Moving with water

Water, as both mirror and an otherworld, is a place beyond judgement. Writer and journalist Lucy Jones in her book *Losing Eden* describes it as a portal to another world. Someone who understands this is Anne Byrne, a professor in sociology who has lived her life by the tides on the west coast of Ireland. A lifelong swimmer since her grandmother taught her when she was a child, and now in her 60s, Anne realizes that swimming in the sea has become her place of belonging and solace. The coastal waters of Galway Bay are where she immerses herself to feel completely energized, recalibrated and balanced.

Anne described the sea as a place we can go to safely and freely to release whatever it is we are feeling, without judgement. "We can't be angry in the water," she said. "It's impossible to feel 'negative', anxious or irritated while in the water. . . water offers respite from ourselves and our thoughts."

Through a deeply embodied practice, Alannah Young Leon and Denise Nadeau invite people to see, listen and experience water as living. In their water workshops, they teach the seven fluid systems in our body: venous, arterial, lymph, cellular, interstitial, synovial and cerebral fluids.[5] There are many other fluids in our watery bodies as well – sweat, tears, saliva and glandular fluids, womb waters and menstrual blood, cervical fluid and semen.

Through curiosity, deep listening, reflective practice and movement, a respectful relationship with water bodies is cultivated. By embodying the water and its characteristics, moving with, in and through water, "water teaches us insights into our local ecology". Revealing stiffness or contraction in our body and helping to soften knots of tension brings fluidity back into our movement.

Water's spiralling motion energizes it, giving it vitality and the ability to receive and transmit information. There are no straight lines in nature, and the spiral is the basic movement and pattern underlying all growth. "What is true for water in nature is true for water in the body," writes Schwenk in his book *Sensitive Chaos*.

Moving is essential for our own vitality to encourage healthy communication within and between every cell in every organ. Circling our head, neck and spine, moving our arms forward and backward in a spiral motion, or rotating our hips, activates and energizes the healing qualities of water in our body, bringing vitality to all of our systems.

That morning on the beach, when I finally let go of the "performance", the feeling of being watched and judged, and began to mirror the movement patterns of the sea birds, waves and tides, I felt an incredible sense of expansion. I moved without any thought, from my neck and shoulders across the length of my extended arms and beyond, into the air that my fingertips brushed, mirroring the fulmar in flight. Still grounded, I felt light, like the wind. As breaking waves rippled up and down my spine, my sense of self became completely fluid. The waterscape I had immersed myself in had transformed my own body of water. As Wong and Christian wrote, "Water continually remakes us, whether we notice it or not."[6] I was beginning to feel remade.

Sensing the flow

Contact with water heightens our sensory and sensuous experience of our world. Scientists studying the effect of natural sounds on the human body are beginning to unpack why the sound of the sea feels so soothing and calming. Ocean sounds act as an antidote to the sharp, shrill, staccato sounds typical of a more urban life, our nervous system working constantly to filter out a cacophony of unnatural noises, scanning for potential threats. Our body reacts with a rise in cortisol, the stress hormone.

The frequency of the constant hum from the ocean flow, the swish and swash of gently surging waves or the more powerful rhythmic pulse of larger breakers all help to stimulate our parasympathetic nervous system – the part of the body that is in charge of rest, relaxation and digestion. This brings on a meditative feeling of calm. It is this multisensory experience, enhanced by the qualities of the sea, that helps us drop more fully into our body. Bringing awareness into our body in this way downregulates a jacked-up or anxious nervous system as our body shifts from "thinking" into "feeling".

Simply put, a feeling is a sensation in or on our body. In our day-to-day lives, so many of us are unaware of how we are actually feeling. According to somatic expert and co-founder of the 360 Emergence, Kate Shela, the body's intelligence is revealed through movement. Water amplifies this because of its multisensory nature. When immersed in a watery environment in some way, especially colder or wilder waters such as the sea, we can't help but notice our body becomes stimulated in new ways.

Water senses us and will interact differently when it senses movement or vibrations of other things, including humans. "We give off these vibrations on a molecular level," Cliff Kapono explained to me. "Water is essentially atoms that are magnetized together in a specific way yet are highly changeable. It has the most interesting atomic structure of any element. Temperature will alter its form, so why wouldn't it be able to renegotiate itself in response to the vibrations of what is around it. Water is always going to find a way to stabilize – to be water. So when a person is introduced to the water, the water is going to feel that and be altered at a molecular level in response to those vibrations."

Patterns of Flow

Flow is the essence of water. Scientist Philip Ball, author of the blog Water in Biology,[7] described how the gigantic flow forms of hurricanes in the ocean as seen from satellite images "illustrate one of the fundamental truths about flow that Leonardo [da Vinci] was seeking to grasp: within all the turbulent chaos of rushing water, there can arise distinct, robust structures and patterns".

These patterns are repeated in art. Leonardo da Vinci, who was also a hydraulic engineer, captured the movement and patterns of water in some of his landscape art. Ball described how Da Vinci's depictions of rivers and streams breaking away into fractal patterns around mountain ranges are like veins of the Earth that resemble the venous system of the human body.

The fulmar, the wind dancer I attempted to embody on the beach that morning, is a Da Vinci of sea and sky. It contains within its consciousness a memory map of the flow of wind patterns and weather systems over open ocean, allowing it to effortlessly navigate the vast deep blue beyond. This seabird is a being that has become part of the fluid elements it inhabits, living an oceanic life beyond horizons familiar to us.

These patterns are also repeated within our bodies. We can activate this inner state of flow if we learn to move more fluidly – like water.

EXERCISE:
FLOWING LIKE WATER

Movement is our first language. In our modern lives so little time is given to full bodied, expressive movement, especially with heightened self-moderation and self-monitoring. Movement allows us to say, feel and express what words can't. In the words of dancer and movement expert Marlo Fisken, "You have permission to unlearn anything that tells you you can't move fully, expressively and with desire and curiosity."[8]

The following exercise is a movement practice inspired by integrating elements from the world of somatic experts and Indigenous scholars Alannah Young Leon and Denise Nadeau and their workshops connecting people with their local water bodies through embodied movement practices. I also draw on the movement practices of director and founder of Dances for Solidarity,[9] artist and choreographer Sarah Dahnke. I met Dahnke during the Flora Fauna Project's collaborative ROOM exhibition – a movement-based arts project during the height of the pandemic. Dahnke creates performance experiences with non-performers or untrained dancers that celebrate the nuances of natural, human movement.

The Dances for Solidarity initiative shares a ten-step movement process through a letter writing campaign with people incarcerated in solitary confinement in the United States. The dance can be interpreted and performed by anyone in solidarity with those behind bars. "Dancing is the most liberating act in the world," wrote one of the incarcerated dance collaborators.

In this exercise you are invited to embody your local water body and its characteristics – to experience water as living. As we move with, in and through water, water teaches us insights into our inner and outer local ecology. "To feel the sacredness of water," Nadeau wrote, "we humans must become fluid and feel our fluidity."

This practice is great to do after the journaling exercise in Chapter 1 or after practising the "Sit Spot" (Chapter 3), where you learn to listen to the water bodies that are significant in our lives through all of your senses.

Move like water

1. Go to your water. If you can't be by water, close your eyes and imagine your favourite water body before you sense it and feel it.
2. Imagine a light warm mist around you; as you move, the mist collects onto your body, filling it with new fresh energy.
3. To release tension held in your body and tap into your innate fluidity, tense every muscle. Hold the tension and count to ten. Now let all of the tension release as you count to ten again, imagining every muscle softening like water. Inhale. Exhale.
4. Sense the movement and depth of the water – how is it flowing, fast or slow? Explore these characteristics with movement: swirling, swishing, spinning, lapping, crashing, exploding. . .
5. Imagine yourself immersed in the water. Soften your body like water. Move however your body wants to move, in

whichever way feels good, always staying connected to the water – twisting forward and back, leaping, swaying, shaking all parts of your body. Inhale. Exhale.

6. Listen to the water – what is it saying? Explore its message with your voice or through sound: slapping, clapping, hissing, roaring, murmuring, sighing. . . Inhale. Exhale.

7. Now imagine you are floating on the surface of the water. Inhale. Exhale.

8. Feel your body grow lighter and lighter as if you are a cloud. Inhale. Exhale.

Open your eyes and give your thanks to the water.

Try this exercise for different bodies of water, such as a stream, river, lake, waterfall or sea.

Turn this into a **group exercise** by bringing one of your water movements, gestures or sounds back for everyone to share:

1. In a circle, share and witness everyone's own expression of water.

2. Move around the circle again, but this time everyone mirrors the movement that each person offers, creating a pattern such as a flock of birds or a wave. Leon and Nadeau called this "flocking". They explained, "Each person's water embodiment develops into a group embodiment, fluidly moving from one water body to another."

CHAPTER 3

EBB

In February 2016, my friend and Hawaiian big wave surfer Brock Little died at the young age of 48. News of his death shocked me. I had not realized he had been so ill with cancer. The photos of him in his last interview in *Surfer* magazine, already a ghost of his former self, knowing he was dying, broke my heart.

All I had were a few scant memories floating inside me like faded butterflies. I needed to create one last memory so I could let go and unhook myself from the dead. To release my grief, I needed to feel a connection, and it felt important that I follow the water's ebb, the withdrawal of the sea from the shore. In 2021, writer Kerri ní Dochartaigh wrote of liminal spaces such as the ebbing tide as *"áiteanna tanaí, caol áit – thin places"*. "These are places," she explained, "where the veil is thin to allow for pauses in the flow of what we know – or think we know – of time."[1] These places feel like they have been set aside for deep, raw solitude.

Several months after Brock's death I had the opportunity to visit the Hawaiian Islands for an artist residency. One evening, I found my way to Peahi, home to the world famous big wave spot also known as "Jaws" that breaks on the largest winter swells. I followed a rough track through scrubby trees and undergrowth down the side of a steep gully to a lively stream below. The water rushed around smooth black boulders on its way to meet the sea, a calm expanse of slate grey that day, and this felt like a fitting place to make my offering, grieve and let go.

I prepared a water offering – a long palm frond I had chosen from my friend's garden, shaped like a Viking longship. Inside it, I placed a pebble from the shore where I first met Brock back home on the west coast of Ireland. Next, I added small white cowrie shells I had beachcombed that morning, and sweetly scented frangipani flowers. Alone, I stepped barefoot into the middle of the stream, balanced on a warm lava rock, smoothed by thousands of years of water flow.

Tears began to stream down my face. Crying cleanses and purifies, literally, by releasing the hormone oxytocin, which can produce a sense of calm, and "feel good hormones" known as endorphins, which help to ease pain in the body, both physical and emotional. In Hawaiian (Olelo Hawai'i), there are over 200 names for rain. *Kauaolelea'anae* rain is the most extreme, and in Kimo Armitage's poetry[2] this is used to express the depth of grief or sadness. That day, *Kauaolelea'anae* were the tears I shed. As I lowered the palm longship into the water, invoking Brock's memory and offering a prayer, a breeze kicked up, swirling around me. Somehow the palm boat followed an invisible slipstream without getting caught in the rocks, and as it approached the sea, a wave rose from the calm waters and took my offering on the ebbing tide, swallowing it whole.

The ebbing tide

I see our relationship with grief closely linked with "ebb". Grief itself is a withdrawing inward, a feeling of emptiness, a surrender to the murkiness, a sinking into what may feel like the abyssal depths of the ocean to be able to feel the fullness of our pain – the true measure of our love and loss. Like grief, ebb is not a state that is held in high regard or honoured much in our modern society of hyperproductivity and overstimulation.

"Never escaping our abundance," Lakota skier Connor Ryan said to me, "has created a sickness and malaise. If the container is always full you'll never value the work it takes to fill it."

In nature and natural cycles, the ebb is as essential as the flow. It should not be mistaken for insulation, cutting ourselves off, or stagnation, which is what happens when we block or suppress emotions. Stagnant water has lost its vitality and life force and has become full of impurities, whereas still water is pure and calm, only appearing motionless because its waters run deep.

As Iranian snowboarder and surfer Starma explained in the previous chapter, ebb is necessary for flow and is a state that allows us to gather our energy for the next phase. The dormancy of winter, when all life above ground appears to have withered and decayed, is extremely important for the health and life cycle of plants and trees. When the leafless deciduous trees appear lifeless, their root system is growing and expanding beneath the earth, strengthening the tree, while the rest of the tree rests. The loss of leaves helps trees conserve water, especially in frozen landscapes, while the deepening of the root system also allows the tree to access liquid water further underground.

The Māori, who have a close relationship with water in all its forms, honour both the ebb and flow of the tide. The Māori calendar is called the Maramataka, literally meaning the turning of the moon, which along with the tides traditionally determined fishing and farming activities. A new moon was considered a good time to fish for eels, which would be out hunting their prey under the cover of darkness using their sensory systems of smell and vibrations, whereas on a full moon the eels would be more wary. Shellfish and seaweed harvesting is best on an ebbing low spring tide.

Ihi Heke, the Maori health and physical activity expert we met in Chapters 1 and 2, explained how lunar and tidal cycles also influence our energy. If we understood this, we would be able to attune our physical activity with the energy of the tides and the natural world. For example, a flooding tide is a good time to do higher intensity cardio. But on an ebbing tide it is better to focus on rest and recovery, he explained. Sometimes the retreat of the sea feels like a loss, symbolizing grief and the longing for the tide to return to wash the pain away.

I have an inner tide that moves me too, identifying certain stages of my menstrual cycle with the ebb and flow of mood, energy and desire. A couple of days after my period I feel a sudden urge for movement and to run, followed by a desire for more explosive and energetic physical activity and strength building at the peak of my cycle (ovulation). I notice how exhausted or depleted I feel if I try to constantly maintain this, being more prone to injury if I push too hard in the second half of my cycle. If I honour my ebb, my body is drawn to expressive, gentle movements, dancing and yoga. As I return to the "inner winter" of my cycle, my body, if I listen to it, demands a sweet surrender – a letting go. I find it much easier to meditate, visualize and do breath work during this phase.

In the surf, how I respond to the ocean and the waves may differ too. In the ebb of my cycle, instead of chasing after waves, constantly roaming up and down the lineup, I am often better able to trust my instincts, timing and positioning, to sit and wait and allow the wave to come to me and then to sense and feel the wave through my body when I ride it. It is when I most honour my inner ebb state that I am able to find moments of flow more effortlessly.

Connor Ryan shared with me a wonderful definition of the value and importance of honouring our ebb. "The thing I think it lends itself to is gratitude and refinement," he said. "Realizing that it's only in this container [of ebb] that, for me, real inspiration arises again. I don't think if I could chase winter all the time around the globe in that space of constant flow, I'd ever really have the ability to recognize the magic of everything happening."

Ebb provides the counterbalance to a hedonistic quest for a state of flow. "You need the contrast," Ryan said, "to realize what's powerful and potent and what's medicine." In his Lakota tradition, ebb reminds him of a vision quest and the need to first fast without water on the mountain, "You have to realize what you are without, in order to really prioritize what it means to have it," he said. "The container is beautiful and powerful, and the work is what it takes to fill the container." And water can act as a beautiful container for our grief.

Water and grief

The unique qualities and properties of water can help us reclaim meaningful ways to be in a relationship with grief and allow healing. In Greek and many world myths, when someone died they journeyed to the underworld, often having to navigate across a body of water or a river, entering a world of darkness. Death is a place of profound certainty and yet total unknowability. It is not unlike how we previously thought about the abyssal depths of the ocean, devoid of life. But even at these tremendous depths, in total darkness, there is life.

American marine biologist and conservationist Rachel Carson referred to the sea floor as "an epic poem of the earth",[3] where all life that ever was is laid down to rest and held and recorded for all eternity. In these sediments we can read all of past history, the arrangement of each and every life through time, reflecting all that has happened in the waters above and from the surrounding lands. The sea bed is an epitaph to all life on Earth.

The association between water, death and immortality is reflected in the myths of many cultures. Water burials were once common for the bodies of chiefs and heroes who were set adrift on rivers and oceans in "death ships". In the Pacific Islands, it was customary to place the dead in a canoe that was launched into the water. These sea burial ceremonies were often carried out to honour a departed loved one, and a variation of this is still actively practised. A canoe with family members carries and returns the ashes of the deceased to the sea with a prayer or chant, while the mourners scatter flower petals on the water to join the ashes drifting in the ocean. These kinds of burials are reserved for those who had an affinity with the ocean or whose *amakua* (spirit guardian or spirit animal) was a sea creature.

In contemporary surf culture, the Hawaiian sea burial has become part of what is called the "paddle out", which, according to most historians, originated at Waikiki beach in Oahu in the 20th century. This is when surfers and others gather together in a floating memorial held in the ocean, close to shore, in tribute to the life and legacy of those they have loved and lost. The surfers arrange themselves on their surfboards in a circle, representing the way the ocean brings people together, and the cycle of life and death. Australian surf scholars Margaret Gibson and Mardi Frost carried out interviews with surfers who participated in paddle-out ceremonies and wrote in their research paper on surfing and the paddle-out ceremony that this ocean-based death ritual "celebrates and acknowledges the human condition of mortality in a nature-based, highly physical, and affective ritual process".[4]

Brock's paddle out was held at Waimea Bay, with hundreds of friends, family and members of the surf community. His surfing performances at Waimea established him as one of the greatest surfers of all time. The Eddie Aikau Big Wave Memorial, or "The Eddie", is the most prestigious surfing contest in the world and is only held if waves reach a consistent minimum height of 20ft (18m). The tournament is held in memory of Hawaiian big-wave surfing legend Eddie Aikau who was also the first lifeguard at Waimea Bay; it is said that he saved over 500 lives during his lifetime.

In 1978, Eddie was lost at sea. He was a crew member on the traditional Polynesian voyaging canoe, *Hokule'a*, on a voyage from Hawaii to Tahiti. About 12 miles off the coast of the Hawaiian island of Molokai, the vessel capsized in the middle of the night. In an act of incredible courage and daring, Eddie decided to go for help and paddled toward the island on his surfboard in the darkness and through the open ocean swells. The crew were eventually rescued but Eddie was never seen again. Some believe that he became part of the ocean waves and his spirit or *amakua* remains in the ocean protecting those who go into the sea.

In 1990, The Eddie was held during one of the biggest swells in living memory, with waves rolling in with 40ft (12m) faces. Aged just 21, Brock paddled into and caught the biggest wave ever ridden at the contest. It was captured in what became one of the most iconic photos of surfing and printed in a double page spread of *Surfer* magazine. It was this image that had bestowed Brock with these mythological warrior-like powers in my mind.

The first time I met Brock was on the sea wall in the surf town of Bundoran in 1995 when he rolled into town with his Hawaiian and Californian pro surfer pals. This was long before surfing was "cool" in Ireland, and Bundoran was still a sleepy, tacky tourist town filled with amusement arcades and slot machines, nightclubs and fast food takeaways. I was nine at the time and it was the first time I saw foreign, professional surfers in the flesh.

I had already heard the rumours that elevated Brock's legendary status in surfing circles even higher. On their way north along the Atlantic west coast of Ireland, Brock and his friends took shelter from the unforgiving elements of a late Irish autumn in a local pub in Doolin. In the half-light of predawn, Brock's friend Brad dared him to paddle to Crab Island. Crab is a famous right-hand wave that peels off the island's rocky reef. Brock paddled out, caught a wave and paddled back, completely naked. As a round trip, the distance is about 1.5km (1 mile). Word spread of his extreme feat of madness/heroism paddling in the nip, immune to hypothermia and surviving to tell the tale. That earned him instant legend status that will live on forever in Irish surfing.

We sat together looking out at the sea and before Brock gave me his autograph, he asked me about my surfing, why I loved it so much, my favourite waves and dreams for future adventures. I told him that someday I would save up enough money to go to Hawaii and surf big, scary, beautiful blue waves. That is when he told me about Waimea, bringing the wave to life. It was his place of encounter. It felt like he was speaking about an intimate relationship, one that both challenged him and filled him full of longing, one that he could not stop thinking about, like he was willing to dedicate the rest of his life to this wave. I was in awe that there could be such a love between a human and a wave.

He handed me back my book after signing it and encouraged me to join them in the surf. I was still a little nervous and uncertain as I had only ridden my first steeply pitching and fast breaking waves over the rocky reef at The Peak that summer, having progressed from the softer, far less intimidating beach break waves of Rossnowlagh. But this was my local wave, so I led the way across the rocky reef on the ebbing tide. Later, I read his words to me: "See you at Waimea Bay, Let's Go Big!"

After Brock died, I wanted to remember him as that Waimea "gladiator of the sea", the "Hawaiian Viking" as others fondly remembered him, referring to both his strong, statuesque presence as well as his tenacious will and drive. He was the first man, other than my father and grandfather, who I had looked up to, who had fuelled my childhood imagination and dreams of adventure, eventually leading me to Hawaii in my late teens to be tested and humbled by his Pacific island waves, including Waimea, although we never did get to surf it together.

Fittingly, a week after Brock's passing, the biggest and best swell in over 40 years hit the Hawaiian Islands, and waves over 70ft (21m) in height were ridden at Peahi. This was where, a few months later, I chose to make my water offering in memory of my departed friend. It was my way to allow grief to move through me and to honour a shared bond with the sea and surfing. Standing in the water seemed to help me acknowledge and retrace my memory space, reconnecting me with the deceased in what surf scholars Gibson and Frost described as "an immersive mode of embodied existence". They wrote that the dead become honoured in a ritual "that releases or places their spirit into a meaningful biographical space". According to Canadian writer Toko-pa Turner, "Grief okays and essentials the role in our coming undone from previous attachments."[5] It is the necessary current we need to carry us into our next becoming.

Releasing our emotions

With the profound sense of release and deep connection following the water ceremony at Peahı, I became more curious about the role water could play in allowing us to process our grief more deeply. I wanted to better understand why water seemed to be so powerful when it came to grieving and releasing powerful emotions, and to learn more about how water environments could help promote healing of emotional trauma or loss.

Neurologist Lisa Shulman, and author of *Before and After Loss: A Neurologist's Perspective on Loss, Grief, and Our Brain*, writes about the impact of loss on the brain. "When we think about brain trauma," she says, "we usually think about physical injury. But we now understand that the emotional trauma of loss has profound effects on the mind, brain, and body. [. . .] Imaging studies of the brain show that the same brain regions are activated by both physical and emotional pain."[6]

We know now that being by water, simply looking at it, can alter our brain waves. When we immerse ourselves, especially in colder, chilly waters, it can feel like a shock at first, and even painful. It has the effect of pulling us powerfully into the present moment by stimulating every thermoreceptor (temperature receptor) in our body. With 3.5 times more cold thermoreceptors than warm ones, this in turn jolts us out of our heads, as if we become aware of our bodily existence for the first time.

Author and wild swimmer Tamsin Calidas called this "a recalibration of our inner compass".[7] Charlie Ryrie, in *The Healing Energies of Water*, explained that colder water is the most receptive and energetically charged. It also has greater density, so perhaps it feels easier to allow the body to surrender to the water – to relax, let go, float and be held.

A few years ago, I met a woman swimming in Galway Bay. She was recently bereaved and described how she sometimes would just go out and roll on to her back and look up at the sky and feel the release. Similarly, Lisa Buckingham, a London-based swimmer, found solace and support in the water after losing her mother to cancer. She shared her experience in an article for *Red* magazine, describing how, as her body sank into the cold, murky water, "it was like someone had jabbed a reset button inside my brain". She shared how she was "jolted back to feeling more normal, less broken". "As my body went into survival mode," she said, "my mind couldn't really focus on anything else and I could have a few blissful minutes of not having to think about loss. As I climbed out, the endorphins kicked in and my shredded nervous system bathed in the feel-good hormones at a time when nothing else felt good."[8]

This healing power of water has drawn so many to it. Water protector Pat McCabe spoke to me about how water was part of her own healing, recovering lost parts of herself, her identity and ancestry. This did not happen until she made her home near the water in the Taos area of New Mexico. "To live across from the springs, I could hear the water running all the time. . ." she said. "I really feel like that water began to wash me. You know water softens; it'll soften stone eventually. So that's what was happening; it was washing all of that other way off me. I give all credit to that water for bringing me back to some kind of natural human state that wasn't about this modern world of competitive, get-rich-if-you-can kind of thing. And that was before I had any ceremonial life."

Water, trauma and therapy

What these stories and experiences all share is how our healing from grief, loss and trauma is felt through our body and our senses. At a time of heightened grief and loss in the world, our connection with water can offer us a powerful salve to heal our wounds.

During bereavement training with Bernardo's, a charity for children's welfare in Ireland, we discussed the potential of surf therapy in working with trauma and grief. The unique combination of water, the novelty provided by the everchanging waves and the rush of adrenaline and challenging environment are all beneficial elements that support embodiment – a full-bodied connection. They all also result in a rewiring of the brain and rebalancing of hormones, which reduces fears and anxieties.

"We live the world through our body," explained environment and health researcher Nick Caddick.[9] His research highlights the benefits of surf therapy for combat veterans who have experienced some of the most severe forms of trauma. One in three combat troops report symptoms of post-traumatic stress disorder (PTSD), but only about 40 per cent seek help. In a study led by Caddick, the experience of surfing for combat veterans grounded them in their physical body, offering respite from PTSD. The sea's constant fluidity and ever-changing quality redirected their consciousness outward, their attention held in thrall by the sensory stimulations of the ocean. Immersion in the waves is a very tactile experience of constant motion, movement and touch. There can also be a cathartic release of emotion when immersed in an environment so much more powerful than the individual self. Veterans reported feeling their troubles being "pummelled out"[10] by the force of the waves.

Surf therapy has been so beneficial to the US Marine Corps that they have worked "ocean therapy" into their

PTSD treatment regime, and the American navy has also invested $1 million into seeing how beneficial surfing can be. Josh Izenberg, surfer and director of the documentary *Resurface*, which explored the power of surf therapy and being in the ocean to alleviate symptoms of PTSD, shared in an interview with *Psychology Today* about why he thought surfing seems to be so effective.[11] Part of this is related to the flow state or being "in the zone". How surfing can keep the focus on the present, demanding a presence and focus that is so singular, there is no room for daily stress and anxieties. Another part is related to the ebb state. The space between the waves, floating in the water in solitude with the ocean or together with other surfers in the lineup looking out to the horizon can create a space of openness and acceptance. During and after the surf sessions, conversations flow more easily, enhancing social connection. Feeling connected to nature can help the body feel emotions that get lost in highly traumatic situations.

We don't need to have gone to war to feel traumatized. Although PTSD is especially prevalent among combat troops and post-war veterans, it affects an estimated three to four per cent of the population[12] (an estimate likely to be much higher following the impact of the pandemic) and can result from a wide range of traumatic events – including physical and sexual violence, childbirth, road accidents and chronic illness. Symptoms of PTSD are often experienced as an exhausting cycle of suffering that dominates everyday life.

According to trauma expert Gabor Maté , our modern society is conducive to creating trauma as it has taught us how not to listen to our body, instead suppressing and defaulting to a chronic state of threat. When we are in this "red mind" state we are only able to perceive "warnings", turning the world around us into a constant threat.[13]

As we learned in Chapter 1, some of the most effective ways of regulating our nervous system, clinical experts such as Stephen Porges argue, are through play and immersion in nature. New experiences and encounters of aliveness help to deepen patterns of connection between our brain, body and environment. As we just learned, immersion in water and experiences such as surfing can facilitate this.

Being immersed in water helps us inhabit a visceral, embodied state, to vividly sense and feel bodily sensations. Connecting with a water environment can support a process of learning how to speak our truth by first beginning to notice our feelings and how they feel in our body. Naming and allowing them, moving our attention to our body and asking what that sensation wants is a process of compassionate inquiry.

Someone who recognizes the power of accessing water in this way and how it can play a key role in trauma-informed care, is Ilwad Elman, who describes herself as a "fish baby"[14] who loves the ocean. She is also a peace activist and human rights campaigner, and works at the Elman Peace Centre that her mother founded in the coastal capital city of Somalia, Mogadishu. The centre works with children in armed conflict and with survivors of sexual and gender-based violence, which led Elman to see an opportunity for ocean therapy to help these young people. Somalia lacks any access to specialized mental health or trauma-informed services, along with the belief that talking about trauma and grief are of little use in a time of survival, but the country has the longest coastline in all of Africa, with vast stretches of white sand beaches and clear water.

Ocean therapy has become an important means of supporting psychological recovery and treating the somatic trauma or stress carried by children affected by war and empowering them with techniques to rebuild and reclaim their lives. This is offered through various beach and ocean activities that support the healing processes. As well as surfing, activities include water meditations and water games. Elman explained in an interview that introducing the kids to the ocean in a therapeutic setting where they surf with a partner helped them to feel safe in the water, "allowing them to trust someone and try to float, to focus on nothing else".[15] She saw how it could create solidarity and community as well as physical activity and psychological support.

Being in the water, Elman said, is an entry point to opening up a safe space and asking, "When's the last time you felt safe in the water? When's the last time you actually laid back in the water and trusted someone to hold you up?" This then creates a dialogue that otherwise wouldn't have been possible. To facilitate this, they hold what she calls "love circles", where everyone enters the water, floating on surfboards or even standing in the water, and holds hands together in a circle.

Feeling the water on the body, the sun on the face, hearing ocean sounds or playing with the water all help to create experiences of "sensory grounding".[16] This grounding in the present can help create a natural sense of ease and engagement with challenging discussions. The novelty of ocean therapy helps to circumvent the shunning of conventional mental health therapies as a western concept that are out of step with local, lived realities. The power of the ocean often appears in Islamic teachings, something that this new approach to therapy taps into. "It is a method that is contextually informed," Elman said, "and will face a higher likelihood of becoming a sustainable and accepted practice of self-care."[17]

During the lockdowns of the Covid-19 pandemic, I began to offer online workshops that used the power of visualization to evoke water memories. I have used visualization as a tool throughout my surfing career to prepare my body and mind for competitions and for the challenging conditions of big wave surfing. The number of days when all the elements might align for a particular big wave spot to break may only happen a handful of times a year. By using neuroimaging, recalling the wave in all its detail through all of my senses, I was able to visualize how I wanted to surf it over and over again.

Visualization is incredibly powerful, as your brain begins to believe that your physical body is actually experiencing what your mind sees. New neural pathways are created linking your brain and your body so that when the big day finally arrives your body can recall the muscle memory and the responses required to ride the wave. Water memories are some of our most powerful memories because of water's multisensory qualities, and water leaves a powerful imprint on our body and mind.

During these online "blue mindfulness" sessions I began to encourage others to recall a personal, positive memory of an encounter with water – an experience that made them feel alive. I invited them to visualize the memory in their mind's eye, recalling it in vivid detail, taking in the richness of the experience through all of their senses – the earthy or salty smells, the feeling of sea spray or wind on their faces, the sound of waves breaking or water running. . . And to notice how being there made them feel. After just a few minutes of being guided through their water memories, there was a profound shift in how each of us felt. We carried some of the feelings from our past encounters with water into the present moment: feelings of calm, peace, relaxation; feeling energized, alive and revitalized; learning to take the ebb with the flow.

EXERCISE:
HONOURING YOUR EBB

The aim of this "sit spot" exercise is simple – to quiet your mind and focus your senses on water. Water has that incredible ability to inspire both movement and stillness. In a fast-paced world, being still by myself sometimes feels difficult but I always find it easier by water. One of my favourite ways to honour my ebb – at times when I feel the pull to go inward, to be alone, when I just want to feel like I am able to land fully in my own body but can't quite figure out how to get there – I practise my "sit spot".

A sit spot is a favourite place you choose outside, ideally by water, where you can be by yourself and cultivate awareness as you engage your senses and notice the patterns of the living world around you. By choosing this one place that you can visit again and again, a quiet yet powerful awareness and sensitivity to water and its influence on all life (great and small) begins to develop and grow. Your sit spot also becomes a place where you can let go of any impulses, urges, anxieties, shoulds or should nots and can instead simply sit and notice and let the world of water fill and enliven your senses.

1. Go outside
2. Find a spot to sit down where you will be relatively undisturbed for at least the next five to ten minutes. The most important thing is to find a spot you can access easily on a regular basis.
3. Take a few slow and deep breaths to relax your body. You might feel unsettled at first, but that is perfectly okay.

4. Practise tuning into all of your senses and observing the water.
5. Move slowly and gently when you are finished. Do not rush away from your sit spot too fast – honour your ebb.
6. Repeat this as often as you can.

You can do this for as little as five minutes, combined with a longer sit spot of 30 minutes when you have more time. Keep it simple, and make it work for you. It is a very simple practice that can leave you with a profound sense of gratitude and deep sense of connection. You may discover that you have already done this without realizing it, but this time you are intentionally connecting with water. Consciously awakening or engaging our sensory abilities helps shift our awareness from our head and our thoughts and into our body, allowing the mental chatter to quieten.

Gently move through each of your senses, observing the water without any judgements or thoughts.

- Listen deeply – the rush of the wind across the water, and the sound of waves lapping or water rolling the stones in a river.
- Drop more deeply into your sense of touch – feel the sun or the damp misted air on your skin.
- Allow your field of vision to expand into the periphery (when you soften your focus your ability to track movement sharpens); alternate this with honing your focus and letting your vision be drawn into the microscopic detail – the beads of water droplets on the wings of a dragonfly hovering above a pool.

- Hone your sense of smell and taste: how wet or dry the air is; the earthy or salty smell of the water.

Once your body has relaxed and your senses have awakened and expanded, you are better able to observe patterns and what these other species (plants, trees, birds and insects) are doing. You are noticing what is present in the environment around you, the life the water is supporting and how it interacts with its environment. Returning to the dragonfly, ask:

- What was it doing?
- Why was it hovering?
- Why was it drawn to the water?
- How does it listen and sense?

Whenever your mind wanders, bring your attention back by focusing on your breath and noticing the water again. This tuning in is what sparks new connections in your brain and creates a feeling of openness in your heart and body. Over time you will notice your state of awareness continue to expand as new neural connections are made.

This practice works best if you return to the same spot every time. It allows an intimacy to build up – noticing patterns through the seasons and the changing mood of this particular body of water. In this way, you are building a relationship with the water.

Through regular practice, the benefits of cultivating this heightened awareness and ability to notice patterns will spill over into your everyday life, including greater capacity for releasing emotions and experiencing gratitude.

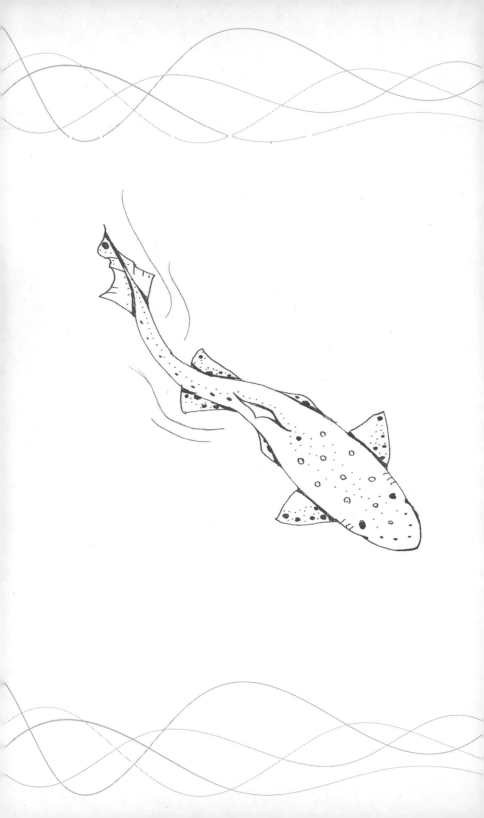

CHAPTER 4

MYSTERY

Much of my work is immersed in the scientific understanding of our relationship with water and how water is as much the object of conflict as it is the source of our healing and salvation, but my interest in water goes far beyond this. Water, to quote author Camille Talkeu Tounouga, "is above all an element affecting humanity's imagination",[1] and is deeply embedded in the mysteries of religion, spirituality, myths, legends and rituals.

Despite the life-giving powers of water, the sea, rivers and lakes were also places of mystery and sources of death for our ancestors. In folklore and mythology, water bodies are commonly portrayed as places to be feared and/or revered. My own name, inspired by one of Ireland's most revered water deities and famous myths, the "Salmon of Knowledge", *an bradán feasa*, is a reminder that there was a time when our ancestors paid close attention to the more-than-human world. They wove the teachings of the sacred salmon into their storytelling, and this continues to be shared today.

The legend tells of the source of otherworldly knowledge that was believed to be held in a sacred Well of Wisdom, which was surrounded by nine hazel trees that were the source of inspiration. The five sacred salmon that swam in the well ate the hazels when these fell into the water, bestowing the salmon with prophetic insight and wisdom, which are powerful symbols in Old

Irish spirituality. Salmon, our non-human ancestors, have inhabited and thrived on this Earth for far longer than we have, evolving some 60 million years ago. Also inherent in the story is a deeply ecological understanding of life, the interconnection and interdependence of all living things. Only recently has conventional science begun to realize this ancient knowing, acknowledging the complex interdependencies between the salmon, the river, the forests and the sea. These interdependencies are explored further in Chapter 5.

Exploring water folklore

Below the beacon of Fanad Lighthouse, at a small table overlooking the sea where the playwright Brendan Behan once sat, I sat watching the waning crescent moon. The moon was in no hurry to set, but its reflection on the gently swelling sea was fading. It hung low over Fort Dunree, which was built in the early 1800s during the Napoleonic wars to guard the entrance to a narrow deepwater bay called Lough Swilly on the north coast of Donegal. The mountain range across the water was starkly outlined by the slow arrival of a winter dawn brightening the sky toward the east. I could hear the water surging and crashing into the rough pink granite rock below.

That day was the feast day of Saint Murgen, an ancient Irish goddess who was once called Lí Ban and is often depicted with a salmon's tail. She is the guardian of the River Bann and its source, Lough Neagh. The river flows into the Atlantic, a little further east from where I was sitting, across an invisible yet potent border with Northern Ireland. The Bann is where some of the first settlers to this island landed over 9,000 years ago, after the great ice sheets from the last ice age had retreated from the land.

A friend of mine, Helen, organized a gathering in Lí Ban's honour to explore her mermaid mythology and how feminine power can influence the emerging future. On the day of the workshop, the first and wildest of the winter storms rose out of the Atlantic Ocean and slammed full of fury into the north Antrim coastline where the event was held. It was as if the angry winds whipping the sea into a frenzy allowed each woman to feel the full range and depth of her emotion. Helen explained to me afterwards how stepping into the raging water felt part of a collective quest to find something beyond the rage. Blindly trusting in a longing for a great sea change, it was also a profound act of love to commit to the intensity of something so raw and wild, their bodies rising up out of the water with the tide and the waves.

Water myths are closely associated with women or feminine energy. Women in the form of mythical female creatures are often depicted as dangerous, violent or monstrous, or when portrayed as beautiful, like the *merrow* from the Irish words *muir* (meaning sea) and *oigh* (maid), they are typically sexualized; their beauty is either a weapon to seduce or a thing to entrap, usually in an unwanted marriage with a human man, an attempt to control or suppress their true nature. Unlike mermaids, the merrow with their seaweed-green hair have humanlike legs but large flat feet and webbed hands for improved movement underwater. Some are said to have sealskin capes that help them swim like seals, a crossover with the *Selkie* myth common across the Scottish Isles, Ireland and even Iceland. Other stories tell of merrows who capture the souls of drowned sailors.

Morgens are another type of water spirit in Irish lore, notorious for drowning unsuspecting men, similar to the Greek sirens with seductive songs that lure men to their deaths. In Slavic regions, *rusalki* are water spirits or nymphs associated with waterways. Once revered as fertility deities in pagan times, worshipped for their ability to help bring forth life, the rusalki came to be portrayed as deadly and dangerous undead creatures during the 19th century. They were believed to be the spirits of young women who had committed suicide by drowning due to an unhappy marriage or who had met a violent death by drowning (usually for being pregnant with an unwanted child).

During Rusalka Week, an ancient Slavic festival also known as Green Week, during the first week in June, swimming was forbidden, for fear that the mermaidlike rusalki would pull you to your death. This portrayal and even vilification of female water deities was not uncommon, especially in patriarchal cultures or during the process of subsuming pagan or Indigenous belief systems into the dominant colonial religions of the modern era. This coincided with the period of rapid industrialization in these regions, including the damming, channelization and modification of many free-flowing waterways.

Other myths associated with water deities and goddesses acted as a warning of the destructive and chaotic power of water, as well as its lifegiving properties. Ceto, a Greek goddess often portrayed as a monstrous figure, symbolized the dangers of the ocean with its realm of hungry, unpredictable sea monsters.

Folklore as protection

Water horse spirits are prevalent in water folklore worldwide, and many stories were used by parents to keep children away from the water to prevent them from drowning. The *kelpie*, very common in Scottish lore, is typically portrayed as an evil water spirit haunting rivers and lakes and often appears as a horse with a soaking wet mane. Some stories tell of how they could shapeshift into the form of a handsome young man who would seduce women and drag them into a watery grave. In their horse form, they appear as cute ponies to children who ride on their backs and are carried into the water to be drowned and then eaten. Kelpies were also blamed for summoning up a sudden flood and sweeping people into the water; the sound of their tail on the water resembled thunder and warned of an approaching storm.

In Inuit mythology, Sedna, who is also known as Arnaqquassaaq in Greenland and many other names by different Inuit groups, is the goddess of the sea or Mother of the Ocean. Many versions of her story exist; in all of them, a terrible act of violence is committed against her yet she transforms her loss into new life. In one version she is dissatisfied with male suitors found for her by her father so she marries a dog. In a rage her father throws her out of his boat and into the sea. When she tries to climb back in he cuts off her fingers which, as she sinks into the depths of the underworld, become the mammals of the sea – seals, walruses, whales and dolphins – which she commands. To ensure a successful hunt, hunters must celebrate and placate her with songs and offerings into the sea so that she might release the sea animals from the ocean.

Artist, author and filmmaker James Houston, who spent many years in the Arctic immersed in Inuit culture, shared his experience of how he saw the myth of Sedna come alive as a way to protect children from the hazardous places around the sea. On south Baffin Island, he wrote, "Some young children were playing near a tidal ice barrier with many dangerous hidden cracks. Their grandmother crept with great care down among the ice hummocks and from a hidden position called out, 'Oohhwee, Oohhwee!' The children ran back onto the land and said the sea goddess Taluliyuk had frightened them. Later, the grandmother said, 'I told them about the woman who lives under the sea. Now she will keep them away from the dangerous places.'"[2]

Arnapkapfaaluk is the fearsome sea goddess of the Inuit people of Canada's Coronation Gulf area. Her name translates as "big bad woman" – the embodiment of the primordial power of the ocean, a warning to anyone who would dismiss its chaos and mystery, and a reminder of the sea's untameable nature.

The paradoxical nature of water, how it can be both protective and dangerous, is a common theme in mythology across cultures. Yemaya was brought from the Yoruba religion in West Africa to the Americas in the 16th century by Africans who had been enslaved. She is an ocean mother goddess still revered in Santeria, an Afro-Caribbean religion. All life is believed to come from her nourishing waters, but if she is not respected she can raise a tidal wave and is known to bathe in the blood of her enemies.

Folklore is not just fantasy or myth but is rich in observation. Water protector Pat McCabe bristles at the immediate tendency to relegate anything that does not scientifically line up with rational thinking. This relationship with the more-than-human taps into parts of human perception that she feels are not welcome in the modern world paradigm. The reclaiming of these stories of our human and otherworldly relationships with water and other beings is seen as one way to restore and heal our lost connection and intimate, ecological understanding of water as the source of life and its multiple lifegiving and leave-taking properties. This is a reminder of the myth and magic we live in every day.

When we welcome these stories, whole worlds open up to us. "Not only does this inform and guide us," said McCabe, "but it's such a joy to have an expanded relationship with all this life around us." She pointed out how Indigenous cultures are always observing and taking on the animals as teachers to help us learn how to be here. She described the different spiritual input that comes from the distinct characteristics of each place, the water bodies and the non-human life that inhabits them. "When I think about Ireland," she said, "I think about the stories of the selkies and the seals." She is curious what that "input" must be like for an individual and also for the community. "When I hear stories of selkies and such, I don't think that's myth," she said. "I think that's exactly the same thing that happens to me with the buffalo [medicine]. . . and I just wonder what was that like?"

In many parts of the world and Indigenous cultures, this knowledge was never dismissed, or what was taken away through brutal and violent acts of colonization is being actively reclaimed and practised once again. "That's why we sail," explained Nainoa Thompson, master navigator of the vessel *Hokule'a* and a member of the Polynesian Voyaging Society, writing in 2009, "so our children can grow up and be proud of whom they are. We are healing our souls by reconnecting to our ancestors. As we voyage we are creating new stories; we are literally creating a new culture out of the old."[3]

Discovering the ocean's mysteries

Anthropologist Wade Davis, in his book *The Wayfinders*, called Polynesia, "the largest culture sphere ever brought into being by the human imagination",[4] covering 25 million square kilometres or almost a fifth of the surface of the Earth, and most of that ocean, with a scattering of thousands of islands. Deliberate and purposeful crossings over thousands of kilometres of the Pacific ocean took place over the course of 80 generations, and led to the creation of a single sphere of cultural life, a culture of navigators, established five centuries before Columbus.

Davis is a friend of Nainoa Thompson, who has trained his whole life to be a navigator. Davis wrote how Nainoa's teacher, Mau, a master navigator from the Caroline Islands of Micronesia, "was placed as an infant in tidal pools for hours at a time that he might feel and absorb the rhythms of the sea".[5] Training as a navigator included not only knowing how to sail but knowledge of "Big Water", the physics and metaphysics of ocean waves, the textures made by the wind on the surface of the sea, the patterns of sunlight on the water, and the meaning of the stars as they rise out of the sea at night on their east–west trajectory, or, as Nainoa put it, the ability to "plot a chart to an island in his mind".

Nainoa prefers the term wayfinder to navigator – setting out to find island archipelagos – and also speaks about using "seamarks" rather than landmarks to find their way. Seamarks could include "a tan shark moving lazily in the sea" or "the flight of a frigate bird heading out to sea", which anticipates calm weather. Following the patterns of other marine species, especially seabirds such as terns and petrels, who have fixed flight routes from their nests out to sea and back again every day, can also aid navigation. Understanding how far each bird travels from land out into open ocean helps wayfinders identify how far away landfall is. Expertly skilled navigators such as Mau can sense and read the refractive wave patterns distinct to each island, long before it comes into view on the horizon, like reading an individual fingerprint. The art and science of wayfinding is the interweaving of all these interactions, insights and intuitions, a holistic and dynamic process of an endless flow of data.

This intimate ecological connection with the coast and sea is something I hear echoed in local stories from Gaeltacht coastal areas in Ireland, beautifully documented in Manchán Magan's cultural *Foclóir na Farraige* "dictionary of the sea" initiative.[6] The Irish language shows just how wide, deep and intimate the knowledge of our forebears was for the living sea, with hundreds of words to describe the changing qualities, moods and patterns of the sea and sea life. There are terms for different types of waves, winds, currents, and seaweeds. This profound understanding of coastal ecosystems and sea knowledge is captured in the word *leamhadóir*, a person who watched for signs for where a shoal of herring was, or *caileantóireacht*, the ability to forecast weather by noticing natural phenomena. Our ancestors could read the weather, using the word for rainbow, *tuar ceatha*, for the sign, omen or portent of a rain shower. It was known how to find the deep water holes where wrasse hide out in the kelp (in areas called *Bráití*), and or how to tell if a ray of light was on the "wrong" side of the sun, heralding the approach of bad weather.

Similarly, in Māori *whakataukī* or proverbs, the shark, Ihi Heke explains, is referred to as "an animal that one should aspire to be like because of its natural desire for life at all costs – the shark does not give up when caught but struggles mightily to the death".[7] Sharks have been around for 400 million years, so what can we learn from the oldest of our ancestors, rather than focusing on fear, revulsion and mass slaughter?

Using art to celebrate the mysteries of water

Irish artist Dorothy Cross's artwork consistently features sharks in a way I had never seen them portrayed before. Once I explained what my book was about, she told me how so much of what comes from water, especially the sea, shapes her work. It is clear that the sea infuses almost all of what she does, where she lives and what she is most drawn to. "From sitting in a bath," she writes in her book *Connemara*, "drinking a glass of water, diving into a pool or sitting on the shore lolling at the ocean. This elemental relationship was at the heart of [my] work."[8]

Dorothy's intimate relationship with water was immediately apparent as soon as I arrived at her home. Her house overlooks the west coast of Connemara and a smattering of inhabited and uninhabited small offshore islands, with all of the front sea-facing windows open and expansive to take in as much of the blue horizon as possible. Stepping into her home I was immediately confronted with a wall-to-wall framed photograph of Dorothy floating in Poll na bPéist, meaning the worm hole or the serpent's lair, the serpent being a symbol synonymous with the sacred feminine, the energy of the goddess, on Inis Mór island. Poll na bPéist is a pool of water thought to be 300m (984ft) deep, cut into a perfect rectangular shape from rock by nature between roiling Atlantic waters and dark, soaring, ragged sea cliffs.

Connemara is a place that painters, artists and writers have been drawn to for centuries, attempting to capture the constantly changing interplay between light, sky and sea. What brought Cross here just over 20 years ago was not so much the desire to create art from this place but instead to explore the depths of the waters around Inishturk, Bofin and Clare islands as a scuba diver. In her book, she described the dark fissures and underwater gullies that trap shafts of sunlight and reefs coated in jewel-like anemones.

Suspended from the ceiling in her studio was a gannet in mid-dive. Like a lot of her work, Dorothy found the gannet on the shore. It washed up dead with a broken neck from hitting the shallow waters at high speed. I imagined Cross with her head bent, scanning the shoreline where the sea meets the strand to seek the detritus of natural and human life washed up on the beach. Other shape shifting items she has found in this space of tidaltime, as she describes it, include whales, sharks, broken boats and jellyfish. She transformed this death and loss into what she called an "inheritance from nature", giving it new and unexpected life in her art.

Speaking about her relationship with jellyfish, and sharks in particular, Cross's whole demeanour shifted. She became more animated and excited, and I could sense her passion as her voice rose and quickened. Her intimate knowledge of these creatures is stunningly portrayed in her work.

"Why jellyfish," I asked.

"That mixture of disgust and desire," she replied, "because when you're under the water with them they are absolutely balletic and beautiful and when you find them on the beach most people are afraid of them. I'm very interested in what most people are afraid of, and what people malign."

I wondered if she could silently sense my own discomfort around jellyfish, which usually trigger a mixture of fear and revulsion in me when I see them in the water, especially stinging ones, and I do my best to avoid them. In the silence that hung for a moment between us, I could almost feel Dorothy daring me to set my prejudice aside and instead embrace the wonder and awe that the world of jellyfish seems to evoke for her. I made a mental note to try to spend more time observing these creatures through this lens.

Jellyfish are almost entirely (98 per cent) water. Cross's fascination for them comes from her obsession and reverence for Maude Delap, another woman whose remarkable life history has been all but forgotten. In 1902, wrote Cross in her book, Maude succeeded in breeding jellyfish in bell jars in her father's house on Valentia Island in County Kerry. She describes how Maude would have waded into the water in her narrow waisted long skirts or rowed out in her small punt every day dragnetting for plankton to feed the jellyfish she was breeding. Using a fish viewer, she would catch a glimpse of the underwater world but never had access to the world of the jellyfish she observed and studied all her life. Had Delap grown up in our time, she may well have joined Cross as she descended through the water to film jellyfish while recording an opera singer singing hymns underwater for one of her remarkable art installations.

Sitting on a low bench in her garden was a bronze cast of an exact replica of a beautiful 2m blue shark called *Everest Shark*. In place of its dorsal fin rose a mountain ridge with the peak of Mount Everest at its centre. This pinnacle of our planet only rose to its great height 60 million years ago. Cross's respect for the sharks comes from the fact that they are one of the oldest animals on the planet, the greatest evolutionary experts and survivors on Earth. Blue sharks' ancestors have been swimming around the planet for over 400 million years, before plants colonized land, and they evolved to their present form 100 million years ago.

Sharks are also among the most feared animals on the planet, the symbol of the fin used to instil fear and terror or the obliteration of oneself. This attracts Cross to the exploration of our own mortality. Each of the sharks she has worked with and transformed into a work of art for her exhibitions all have a story, and she has found them in different ways and places.

"One, I bought in a market with a friend who runs a restaurant," she said. "He took the meat and I took the skin." Cross skinned the porbeagle shark and pickled the skin herself in her studio in Connemara. To celebrate the shark's beauty and value, she lined the inside of its skin, the cavity where its body once existed, with pure gold. She called it *Relic*, transmuting it into the sacred and holy. Now, thankfully, sharks are no longer sold for their meat in Ireland.

Cross's work is a collaboration *with* nature. "It's about respect, and it's all about relationship, she said. "My relationship with you, to him [she pointed to Connie, her dog], the ocean. The importance of all those relationships which we are being further and further removed from, with health and safety, with sanitation, with pollution – all those things. Is that progress? Some would say it is but I don't particularly think it is."

It is also true that it is possible to change our relationships with nature for the better. The *Basking Shark Curragh* is another of her artworks now hanging from the rafters of her studio. It speaks to a time when we once hunted basking sharks in curraghs, small traditional Irish seagoing boats to near extinction for their oil. The oil from sharks and whales was used as fuel in street lamps and to light up the first lighthouses all around Ireland and the British Isles in the last century. Later, sharks and whales were hunted for their rich source of squalene, an oil extracted from their enormous livers, to use in industrial lubricant and as a moisturizer in cosmetics. It seems bizarre and unsettling to imagine rubbing the remains of such a wild and ancient creature into the lines of my face, slowly aged by the same sun and sea that the shark so loved to bask in, or that these creatures ended up literally oiling the wheels of industrialization, hastening the demise of the ocean itself. Today, basking sharks are legally protected in Irish waters.

Cross's *Basking Shark Curragh* is about being held safely – the skin of the shark saving your life if you are out in the ocean within the vessel, the shark's fin functioning almost like a rudder, providing direction. Belmullet and Achill islands just across the bay thrived economically on the shark industry. Now the roads on Achill Island to Keem Bay are blocked with traffic jams during the summer, with people hoping to spot a basking shark swimming on the sea surface in the nearshore waters.

Cross had asked the Irish Whale and Dolphin Group to let her know when one was found stranded as this is a rare occurrence. "Sadly we found one and skinned it on a beach in Wexford and it weighed a ton," she said. They put it in a car and returned to Connemara

Dorothy believes it is impossible for art to capture or explain nature. Nature is a force that exceeds the framing of both art and science, and yet it is never something we are separate from; we are wholly immersed in it.

"Let's run down to the sea, will we?" Cross asked me, and I didn't have to be asked twice.

We headed down the road for a few miles until we came to an old famine road dating from at least the 1800s, a rough grass-covered track that once would have run from the valley behind and up to the commonage on the mountain top, down the other side and all the way down to the sea. This would have provided people in the valleys with access to seaweed to fertilize their crops, and people at the coast access to the upland bog to cut turf to fuel their fires. The bottom of the track opened up to breathtaking views of the beach and the bay beyond leading into Killary fjord where Mayo's largest mountain, Mweelrea, rises.

Cross led me down to the rocky shore and showed me a hidden waterfall that plunges 30 feet into a cavern in the rocks, like a temple, or "a good place to wash your hair when you had no house," she told me, laughing. At low tide, when the sea is calm, it is possible to enter through a cave on the seaward side and reach the foot of the waterfall through a crack in the rocks. She likes to go there alone, take off her clothes and swim in the sea. I breathed in the fine mist created by the falling water, reminded of its healing potency and hoped it would provide my lungs with an added layer of protection for the winter to come.

A painting I once did of Mamala came to mind when I heard Cross share her reverence and joy for that place and the pleasure it gives her. Mamala is a Hawaiian *kupua* or spirit entity as well as a chieftess famous for her wave-riding skills. She has the ability to shapeshift into whichever form she most desires. Sometimes she chooses to appear as a shark or half shark, and other times riding a shark. Cross is often not alone while she is there. Otters sometimes swim up the streams that criss-cross her land from the sea. She said they follow the network of streams and go over the hill and across the bog to a lake hidden from view above the walled gardens of Kylemore Abbey.

Mysteries of the ocean depths

On the drive back home I began to think about the waterfall, the streams that appeared out of the ground all of a sudden and hidden bog lakes on mountain tops – the waters all around us that we can't see, as well as the water held deep in the ocean. Once considered an empty void, the deep ocean is home to such a surprising diversity of life adapted to the extreme pressure, cold, dark, oxygen-deprived environment. This hidden, unknown "otherworld", a place of perpetual darkness, also referred to as the "abyssal zone" was brought into people's homes and living rooms all across the planet in the second episode of *Blue Planet II* called "The Deep". The stunning documentary revealed just how awe inspiring the deep is.

Director Orla Doherty captured many of the mind-blowing never-seen-before images of this underworld, including ancient six-gilled sharks feasting on whalefall, a sunken whale carcass; *Phronima*, a parasite that inspired HR Giger's chest-bursting alien; ethereal hadal snailfish found at 7,200m (4½ miles) deep; and mythical-looking underwater lakes, or brine pools on the sea floor. The extremely high salinity and lack of oxygen at these brine pools make them toxic to most organisms. Yet, even here, there is life specially adapted to the "shores" of these lakes – various bacteria, microorganisms and eels that dive in and out for quick swims, an abundance of life in the most inhospitable of environments, with hot air vents belching methane and other toxic gases and intense heat. New species are being discovered, such as the Dumbo octopus recorded during the first *Blue Planet* series. Marine life believed to occupy only the upper surface of the ocean, such as manta rays, swordfish and mako sharks, were found at incredible depths in the twilight zone moving between the layers of the ocean's underworlds for reasons we can't yet comprehend.

Watching it all, it could be easy to believe that there remains a part of the world full of magic and mystery untouched by humans. But it is no longer true that the ocean remains impenetrable to us, even if it remains out of our reach and we can't see or sense it. Human impacts are felt even at depths of 3–6km (2–4 miles), where no human has ever been. When the life contained in the ocean dies and decays, it begins its slow descent to the ocean sea floor, like gently falling snowfall.

"When we are wise enough, perhaps we will read in them all of past history."[9] Marine Biologist Rachel Carson wrote these words in her 1951 book, *The Sea Around Us*, just before we entered the era of single-use plastics, creating a throwaway culture that persists to this day. She was right – we can indeed read all of past history in the sediments of the deep.

In the deposits of these successive layers of sediments, we now find the colourful, deadly composition of everyday items of our human lives, such as plastics. All life has evolved here to feed on the detritus of the ocean, and these species try to eat the plastics, which are full of toxins instead of nutrients. Other pollutants, the effects of climate change and ocean acidification can also be felt in the abyssal zone, reducing the already limited abundance and diversity of life. On top of this, overfishing further reduces the "snowfall" of dead organisms that Carson wrote about, the preferred food source of the creatures of the deep.

We have drowned the mysteries of the ocean with our artificial noise, from shipping, deep sea mining, oil extraction, sonic booms and military testing. The interference from all these activities can be felt in every part of the ocean, disturbing the social order of all life underwater. While, at the same time, the natural sounds of the ocean grow quieter with the rapid loss of the abundance of marine life, which changes the sound of the sea. Imagine how the ocean would have sounded when millions of whales from possibly hundreds of different species, many of which no longer exist, swam in the seas, each with their own unique way of making sound.

The power of water rituals

Does the ocean still hold a sense of wonder if it is no longer full of mystery but is littered with the familiar debris of human life? Rebecca Giggs argued in her book, *Fathoms*, that for many of us the ocean is a powerful psychological motif. What will it mean for our inner lives, she asked, when no part of the ocean remains "untouched" by our human presence and when all aquatic life is in constant relationship with the unwanted waste of our consumer culture? How can it mirror the unknowable space of our unconscious, evoking awe and wonder? The despoliation of the ocean, Giggs argued, corrodes our imagination.[10] With so much loss we are creating a deficit in our language and culture.

One way to restore this deficit is through the cultivation of deep listening, engaging in ecological dialogue. Rituals were created, in part, as a powerful way to listen more deeply, often through attunement with our bodies and the rest of the living world. They offer ways to reignite our imaginations and reclaim the dreaming space that Iranian snowboarder Starma talked about – how the ocean shows up in her unconscious dreaming world. "I always had a dream of diving into the ocean, putting my head inside the ocean and seeing and listening to other species, whales and dolphins since childhood," she shared with me. Since learning to surf, the ocean shows up in her unconscious at least once a week.

It is perhaps unsurprising that so many rituals for various rites of passage and in honour of important transitions in the cycle of life from birth to death, involve water. After the breakdown of her marriage, and as a mother with two small children, water protector Pat McCabe sent out a call – "I need help. . ." – and was invited to her first Lakota sweat lodge ceremony. "It changed everything," she told me. And she has now been on that road for the better part of 30 years.

In that first ceremony, a very specific one named Inipi, one of the biggest aspects for Pat was what she called embodied prayer, an act that purifies, especially after so much oppression of bodily needs and sensations. It purifies not only the skin but also the patterns in our minds and emotions, she says: "It can interrupt the tracks of emotions and change it so you have the opportunity to live in a completely different mindset and heart set." The principal way that happens is by pouring water on hot stones, with the steam becoming the conduit for healing and for spiritual interaction. "'Steam is the breath of your creator,' my sister always told me," Pat said. Fire is used to heat the stones for the Inipi, and she was told "no hard mind at the fire". She believes the same is true of the water: no hard mind; no place for opinions or debate. A place beyond human consciousness.

Chalchiuhtlicue is the Aztec goddess of water, lakes, rivers, seas, streams, storms and baptism and is the patron of childbirth. Her association with water and fertility speaks to the Aztecs' association with the womb and water. She was invoked by priests who would dive into a lake and mimic aquatic life, such as the croaking of frogs, in the hope of bringing rain. At birth, a ritual was performed to honour the water goddess by midwives using water to purify and protect the newborn child. As soon as the baby was born, the midwife would pour or sprinkle water on the head of the child, saying a prayer that recognized water as the divine source of all life since the beginning of the world. She would pour water on the chest of the baby, the celestial water washing impurities from the heart. The water was given to the newborn child so that it may wash away all misfortune. Finally the midwife would wash the entire body of the baby, washing away any unhappiness that may be hidden in the body by saying, "Today, she is born again in the healthful waters in which she has been bathed, as mandated by the will of the goddess Chalchiuhtlicue."

Listening to water

The recognition of the transformative power of water from the moment we are born helps to renew our connection with it. Perhaps the "rewilding" of water begins with the rewilding of ourselves. Empathic prayer that Pat spoke of is one possible way to heal the sense of separation from the natural world that persists and pervades so much of our modern, everyday lives. Another name for empathic prayer, the kind of prayer my grandmother also practised, could also be called embodied listening.

As I learned from Lakota skier Connor Ryan, the only way to listen deeply is to cultivate these personal relationships that we have with places. This growing place–connection informs our listening ability and our ability to recognize the patterns that nature keeps presenting to us. One way to do that is to practise the "sit spot" exercise in the previous chapter, or use the listening practice I share at the end of this chapter. Imagine becoming so intimate with the mysteries of a place, with water, that you could discern the type of woodland you are in by the sound the raindrops make when they fall.

Botanist Robin Wall Kimmerer wrote in her book *Braiding Sweetgrass* about the different types of raindrops that form in relationship to the terrain and plant life they come into contact with as they fall. She gave the example of the difference between raindrops that collect and fall from a fir tree to the raindrops that land first on the broad leaves of a sycamore. The rain from the sycamore falls bigger and heavier, making a different sound. Alder trees, she wrote, "make a slow music".[11] The next time it rains, receive it as an invitation to listen and to hear what music the rain is making.

There are different ways of listening to water. In Japan, wells and springs were important public gathering sites, and within Japanese households the sound of water was always integrated into the design of private gardens. *Wave Rings*, an interactive art installation, seeks to evoke the value of water for communication in public spaces in Japan once again. The structure is designed to encourage participants to communicate with each other by using sounds that create rings in the water – instead of language, using the patterns of water to communicate.

The River Listening project, directed by soundscape ecologist Leah Barclay, records the changing soundscapes of river systems and brings them into local communities, engaging them with the otherwise unknown, mysterious world beneath the surface of the water. Using simple hydrophone technology, Barclay engaged with other scientists as well as artists and musicians. The project began in Australia and has since spread around the world, comparing the sounds of remote, free flowing rivers (a rich, varied, textured cacophony, or rather symphony, of pitch and resonance), with dammed or polluted rivers (literally silent). This method of listening has also become an important, non-invasive way of monitoring (or listening to) the health of a river ecosystem. As a result, "sound walks" have been created as ways to re-engage communities with their local waterways, walking in a way that your feet become your ears, as Barclay described during a talk she gave as part of the River Guardian online training. Listening with your whole body, creating empathic prayer.

My own empathic prayer

Mystery is best felt through the body, not by trying to analyze the world around us through our thinking mind. Water, for me, has always spoken to my body. I can hear it calling whenever I remember to pause and quiet my mind enough. My body knows when it needs water to quench its thirst or to feel renewed and replenished. The experience of mystery is also felt most strongly when the light of the day is fading or has not yet fully returned, at dusk or dawn, when our senses are heightened and bodily instincts kick in. The following is a time when I felt I came close to experiencing the mystery of water.

It was dusk, and I was moving across the boggy ground, sensing it sink, shift and squelch beneath my bare feet despite the lack of rain in recent days. In contrast, the heather was dry and springy. I reached a stream tumbling down the side of the mountain. Feeling my thirst, without a vessel to drink, I crouched and lowered my face to the water, sipping it through my lips, lapping the sharp, cold fluid into my mouth with my tongue. I noticed the earthy acidic taste of the ancient bog oak mingled with the sweetness of the heather and, crouched on all fours, felt my animal self rise to the surface. . . A short way downstream, the torn, discarded remains of a bird on the bank took me by surprise – feathers, bone and blood scattered by the stream tumbling down the side of the mountain. I was struck by both the violence and the ordinariness, the "just-is"ness, of the scene: my repulsion and fascination of death feeding life.

Further downstream in the soft, pale, grey light from a fading autumnal sun, I slowly stripped off and sank into a pool of cold mountain water. Like a holy water font designed to shape the contours of my body, it was just large enough to contain me as I submerged my whole self, my head beneath the surface. I remained in this place in between, a very thin place, for as long as my one breath allowed. I felt the fierce sting of the cold in my chest, before surfacing and sucking in a lungful of crisp, clean air, my ribcage and world expanding. This was my prayer.

EXERCISE:
UNLOCKING WATER'S MYSTERIES

This "sonic water practice" helps to create an ecological dialogue with water or a waterscape through deep listening and sound exercises. You can do it wherever you find the movement of water outdoors, such as taking a moment to pause in the woods when it is raining, sitting by a river, on a boat in a lake or when walking along the coast. It is inspired by the work of sonic meditation expert Pauline Oliveros and soundscape ecologists such as Leah Barclay.

1. Begin by observing your breath.
2. Come into stillness with yourself and gently close your eyes.
3. Become aware of all the sounds of the waterscape – the surrounding environment and elements, until you feel saturated with all these external sounds.
4. Gently cover your ears to block out as much of the external sounds as possible, listening carefully to the internal soundscape of your body – your heartbeat, breath, blood pressure, nervous system. . .
5. Once you feel fully connected with the sounds of your inner landscape ("inscape"), open your ears again.
6. Let the sounds of the waterscape mingle with your inscape.
7. Bring your awareness to a single source of sound from the waterscape around you.

8. Gradually begin to reinforce the pitch of the sound source or its resonance with your own voice or body. Rather than mimicking, reinforcing is a strengthening or sustaining of the pitch.
9. You may wish to hum, sing, make any kind of vocalization or sound with your body, all the while maintaining awareness of the source of the sound.
10. If you lose the source of the sound, come back to the breath and stillness until you can find it, or another sound to be with, and reinforce again.
11. Practise this for as long as you like.
12. You may also wish to imagine how the water is receiving your sound, and what other sounds may remain beyond your aural reach just beneath the surface.

Creating this kind of resonance, through deep listening and the use of sound, especially humming, is also a powerful way to activate our ventral vagus nerve, helping our body reach homoeostasis (relative stability), calming our heart rate and downregulating our nervous system.

CHAPTER 5

POWER

Water is a source of tremendous power. When understanding our relationship with water and how we might restore it, it is necessary to consider what is meant by "power". "Power over" is the form of power that uses force, domination and control, with power over systems creating division, separation and binaries of opposing forces. When applied to water this results in the damming, diverting, draining and polluting of water; it is about the conquest of water, where even something as seemingly invincible as ocean waves can be impacted by humans. Under this form of power, even the waves need saving.

The damming of rivers

Over 70 per cent of the world's large river systems no longer flow freely, having been dammed and diverted. In Europe, only 12 per cent of all rivers remain free flowing. The damming of rivers severely threatens their capacity to share their gifts of water, food, flood control, biodiversity and recreational health benefits. The longest free-flowing rivers (over 600 miles long) are found in the most remote regions of the world, although they may not remain that way.

In the world's largest river basin, the Amazon, there are already 158 dams under construction or in operation with plans to build 500 more. This not only completely alters the entire ecosystem, but the dams are built primarily on Indigenous land where thousands of communities have been illegally and forcibly displaced. According to the analysis, there are currently 60,000 large dams worldwide. In just the Balkans region of eastern Europe alone, there are 3,000 hydropower plants in the pipeline, according to a report from the Save the Blue Heart of Europe campaign group.[1] Nearly 1,500 of these dams are in protected areas and national parks, and these are in addition to the more than 1,000 that already exist.

Migrating populations of fish such as salmon often completely crash after rivers are dammed. "When a dam is put in," said Herman Wanningen, an aquatic ecologist and creative director of the World Fish Migration Foundation, in 2021, "the free-flowing river suddenly becomes a stagnant reservoir, the natural habitat disappears and with it the fish."[2]

Since a hydroelectric dam was built on the lower part of the river closest to my home, the Erne, in the 1940s, the river has now become a virtually salmonless river system, compounded by the decline of wild salmon seen in all waters. Since the last small-scale salmon drift-netting fishery closed for good in 2010 in Ireland, local fishermen at the time remarked on the loss not just of their livelihood but of the knowledge about the salmon.

"You had to know the coast, you had to know the rocks, you had to know the tides," one fisherman told me. He added that in 10 years' time, "nobody will know the coast as well as the salmon man did. You've lost all the information too."[3] Who will care then, he wondered, when the last wild salmon is gone – will anyone even notice?

The synchronicity of salmon

My relationship with rivers began early. The first time I surfed over rocks was at my namesake, a surf spot called Easkey Left, when I was nine. The wave wraps around a small headland and folds into an inlet at the mouth of the River Easkey. The shape of the coastline and current of the river has formed a bank of rounded stones that causes the wave to peel consistently toward the shore in one direction, hence the "Left".

The first settlers to this island were undoubtedly drawn here by the abundance of wild Atlantic salmon. It is surely no coincidence that two of the earliest settlements were at Mount Sandel near the estuary and on the banks of River Bann on the north coast and at Inis Saimer at the mouth of River Erne on the northwest coast, among the island's most important salmon rivers.

The Easkey River no doubt supplied the residents of Roslee Castle, strategically built at its mouth in the 13th century, with a plentiful source of food. It remains very popular with anglers today, although there is a catch and release policy on many Irish rivers and some are closed to fishing completely, in an attempt to conserve the dwindling numbers of salmon returning to spawn in their native rivers after spending up to four years roaming the open ocean. The numbers of returning salmon have dropped from over 30 per cent in the past to as low as 3 or 4 per cent in recent years.

Surfing there, the water feels colder than anywhere else, and less salty, with the mixing of fresh golden-coloured "sweet" water carried from the peaty upland bogs by the river into the saltwater of the Atlantic Ocean. Salmon have an incredibly intimate, finely tuned relationship with water. Remarkably, they have evolved and adapted their upriver migration to the particular qualities of water, harnessing its vitality to leap waterfalls and reach their spawning grounds. Their power to leap is only possible when water is at its peak energy – not too hot, but when it is cooler and able to freeflow. The fish use vortexes of energy, the spiralling pattern of flowing water, to propel themselves upward. The colder the water, the more vitality it has. Water is at its most dense at 4°C (39°F), and at its optimum vitality, making it easier for the fish to swim upstream, while the shape of the salmon's bodies allows the water to flow around them in a spiral.

Warming water temperatures in rivers and seas can have serious consequences for all marine life, especially fish. It is believed that even a warming of 0.1°C (-18°F) disrupts the salmon's usual patterns. In Europe, temperatures in our rivers are expected to increase by 1.6–2.1°C (34.8–35.8°F) on average before the end of this century.

Through their close dependence on water and fishing for survival, these early human settlers must have observed the natural intelligence of the salmon, their unique life cycle and how finely tuned they are to the natural biorhythms of the local river and coastal ecologies as well as having the ability to sync with seasonal changes in temperature and water flow. This dependency creates a more intimate connection and the development of keen observations and ecological knowledge through generations.

What happens when that connection is lost – when communities are not only no longer in direct contact with their food source but with the source of something so free flowing and wild? Is that why freshwater ecosystems are the world's most degraded and are under threat like never before? If rivers are the arteries of the planet and they are being dammed, diverted, drained and polluted, what cost must that have to us and to Earth's living systems?

A river's powerful connections

Another early memory of a direct encounter with the power of a river was when I was 11. I was following the Trisuli River close to its source in the Himalayas, while my mum and I were travelling in Nepal. The water was milky coloured as it cut deep canyons through the green foothills north of Kathmandu in Nepal and would later join the Narayani River, a tributary of the mighty Ganges.

The source of the Trisuli lies in Tibet, far from the sea, and is the heart of the region's water supply for billions downstream. The Trisuli is also one of the most popular rivers in the region for white water rafting. Travelling by water opens up an entirely different perspective on a place. My memories from that time return in intense flashes, leaving a powerful imprint in the memory cells of my body.

Each day was full of possibility, and the unexpected was always to be expected. I have vivid memories of camping by the water, on fine white sand, where it pooled in a bend in the river making it safe for swimming. A woman from a nearby village with her hair wrapped in a red shawl sat quietly on the rock next to my mum, both watching their children play – the shared bond of water and motherhood, the universality of mixing water with play.

All these elements stirred up by the river created a visceral, cross-cultural connection. I remember my wonder at how Noresh, our river guide and Sherpa, could cook up a chocolate cake over a campfire, his laughter like playful water rapid bouncing over rocks, and my wariness of stepping on scorpions in the night when leaving my tent to take a pee in the bushes. I would lay my head down by the river's flow to fall asleep at night to the tinkling, bell-like sound as the shallow water bounced over rounded stones with the deeper constant hum of distant rapids in the background.

That journey to Nepal at such a young age opened me to the light and dark of the world – a place where life and death coexisted and were celebrated, nearly always intermingling with water in some form. Milk was used to cleanse the dead and blood was used to cleanse the living. The names of the rivers ran over my tongue like a sacred, magical text: Trisuli, Kali Gandaki, Narayani, Bagmati. . . The memories feel like the fine spray that hangs in the air after navigating a rushing rapid.

The river connected such an unlikely mix of people, serving as transport, recreation, inspiration, purification, life force, bathing, laundry, birthing water and conduit to the afterlife. At the holy city of Pashupatinath I remember witnessing my first cremation. The body was covered in a blazing fabric the colour of sunset, mourners casting flowers and offerings onto the pyre before it was lit on a platform that jutted out into the Bagmati River, the blaze of the fire engulfing the body reflected in the water. Upstream, other families were busy washing clothes and bathing.

It seemed the boundary between the living and the dead was very thin, all part of one cycle with one flowing into the other – water having the power to bring forth life, to purify and cleanse, and to take life away. Nearby, an ancient stone sculpture of a sleeping god, Vishnu the Supreme Being, was bathed in an ocean of milk. The milk flowed into the river, fanning out into a white plume blessed by a deity.

Since that time, the upper reaches of the Trisuli have been dammed multiple times, harnessing its raw power for hydroelectricity. I do not know how that has affected the flow or the communities that we met along its riverbanks all that time ago.

Harnessing water's power

The glaciers of the Himalayas represent the third largest deposit of ice and snow in the world, after Antarctica and the Arctic. The estimates for the number of people dependent on the rivers and glaciers there – as a water source for drinking, agriculture and hydropower – range from 1.3 billion to 1.9 billion.[4] Temperatures have risen 1°C (-17°F) since 1975 and continue to rise. The difference between water and ice, changing from a solid to a liquid state, is one degree. Since 2000 to 2016, ice loss has been accelerating with rising temperatures, and billions of tons of ice have already melted, with as much as a quarter of ice lost in the last 40 years.[5]

According to the International Centre for Integrated Mountain Management, at least one-third of the Himalayan glaciers will disappear by the end of the century even if countries entirely curb their greenhouse gas emissions by 2050.[6] All of this comes at a time when Nepal is experiencing a hydropower boom to meet its growing energy crisis, with rolling blackouts lasting for up to 14 hours at a time. Despite this, all the evidence points to the inadequacy of hydropower as a sustainable, longterm, viable means of meeting energy demands.

In America, where nearly every stretch of major river has been dammed, with over 80,000 dams of all sizes, 69 dams were removed in 2020 in an attempt to help restore the rivers. As Europe and America are decommissioning dams that failed, and with international movements underway to "free rivers", foreign investment has shifted to developing nations, with thousands of dams proposed or under construction, threatening to reduce free-flowing rivers worldwide by up to 25 per cent.

Hydropower dams are framed as "sacrifices" in the name of sustainability and the "green economy". But there is nothing "green" about them, especially when it comes to generating "clean energy". Hydropower has also proven to be highly inefficient at generating energy, with extremely high environmental and social costs. In a high-risk zone such as Nepal, the volatility of water supply and flash flooding from glacier lake outbursts and reduced water availability pose additional challenges.

The non-profit organization Save the Waves International was established by concerned surfers to fight legal battles to try to "save the waves". Other forms of power can help to restore our relationship with water, if we recognize that power is not something that can be wielded but rather, like water, is a fluid, dynamic balance of forces and energies in relationship with each other. "Power with" is the kind of power that helps to foster collaboration and collective action – that fuels the movements of the water protectors and river guardians and organizations such as Save the Waves. "Power to" recognizes water's own innate power and potential to create and entirely reshape life.

The most powerful river in the world is the Amazon, discharging eight trillion gallons of water every day. The tides are so strong at the river's mouth that they create the largest tidal bore in the world, *the Pororoca*, with waves up to 4m (13ft) high marching up the river for as much as 800km (497 miles) on the largest tides of the year during the spring and autumn equinoxes. There is also tremendous kinetic energy in ocean waves. One of the largest waves ever recorded measured 28.1m (92ft) on a wave buoy just off the coast from my native Donegal in the North Atlantic during the winter I was writing this book. That height is greater than a six-storey building.

To predict the increasing intensity of coastal storms due to climate change, scientists are researching historical and recent "inundation signatures" that storms leave on the coastline. Essentially, these are large deposits of coastal boulders, some the size of double-decker buses or even bigger, that indicate the force of the sea and storm waves. These boulders can be found on top of the highest cliffs, flung up there by waves shooting up the cliff face. "Power within" recognizes a person and a non-person's self-worth and self-knowledge; the ability to celebrate the beauty of our differences, to see water as the life blood that connects us all.

"Power over" dominates industrialized societies, leaving a wake of destruction. The environmental costs associated with traditional dams include the disruption of fish migrations, severe damage to water quality, increased water temperatures, reduced flow, the flooding of richly biodiverse riparian habitat and a severe strain on a river basin's overall water budget.[7] The drastic reduction of sediment load leads to the loss of river deltas and impacts nearshore waters – the nursery grounds for aquatic life and the crucial link between marine and upland water ecosystems, worldwide, altering the water cycle.

In the face of increasing droughts and more severe flooding globally, the health of rivers and our relationships with them are a community's first line of defence. Our attempt to control the flow of water and the drastic mismanagement of water systems leaves us ill-prepared to cope with the pressures of the climate crisis. Hydro dams are a type of technology that is not designed to help the Earth but rather "to maintain this way of living at the expense of the Earth".[8] According to a study by leading scientists in *Nature* in 2019, only 23 per cent of rivers longer than 1,000km (621 miles) flow uninterrupted to the ocean.[9]

The loss of free-flowing rivers means we lose the many benefits that healthy river ecosystems provide. These benefits can't be reduced crudely to "ecosystem services" but instead should be considered to be the lifeblood of the planet. In the same way that blood in our arteries transports energy and nutrients to every cell in our body and the flow of blood in our veins cleanses toxins, so do our rivers, renewing life on the planet. Constructing a dam and blocking the flow and connectivity of river systems is the human equivalent to a blocked artery. If considered in this way, the Earth's beating blue heart is at serious risk from cardiac arrest.

Social injustice of power

These feats of engineering are rooted in power and control over waterscapes, women, Indigenous peoples and other minorities, and have serious implications for future resource extraction and possibilities of creating a just "blue economy". The social and cultural drawbacks of all this are as severe as the environmental drawbacks and are not mutually exclusive. This rush to gain control and to block up and extract from the last free-flowing rivers is associated with conflict, high levels of corruption and the forceful eviction of thousands of entire communities.

Dr Leah Temper leads a team of scientists, activists, lawyers and citizens working to create the ever-evolving global Environmental Justice Atlas with an inventory of socioenvironmental conflicts and resistance, especially where rivers are concerned. According to Dr Temper, and clearly evidenced by the atlas, hydropower has a long history of systemic repression and is one of the most violence-triggering activities. Up to 10 per cent of hydropower cases result in the death or murder of activists. The atlas includes information on dams and water-distribution conflicts, helping to expose criminalization and violence, share successful resistance and river restoration strategies and highlight transformative alternatives.

The control of access to clean water is another form of power over marginalized communities. Safe water, poverty, racial and gender inequalities are all inextricably interlinked. Currently, 748 million people live without access to safe water and 2.5 billion live without adequate sanitation.[10] This is a shocking yet not unsurprising figure considering that 80 per cent of all waste water is discharged – largely untreated – back into the environment, polluting rivers, lakes and coastal areas.[11] Water as the universal solvent, with the ability to dissolve nearly all substances, is also what makes it so susceptible to pollution. It is staggering to realize that unsafe water kills more people each year than war and all other forms of violence combined.[12] According to the most recent surveys on national water quality from the US Environmental Protection Agency, nearly half of rivers and streams and more than one third of lakes are so polluted that they are unfit for swimming, fishing and drinking.

In the last 50 years we have lost 30 per cent of all freshwater ecosystems, and the remaining ecosystems are the most polluted and degraded in the world, with one in three freshwater species now threatened with extinction. Natural wetlands have been harder hit, with global figures estimating the disappearance of over 70 per cent of these habitats in the last century as a direct consequence of human activity (draining, diverting and "reclaiming" for industry and development).

Whenever there is a water crisis, marginalized, low-income communities are hardest hit, especially Indigenous, First Nations, black or other ethnic minorities. A study in the United States by DigDeep and the US Water Alliance found that race is the strongest predictor of water and sanitation access. Flint, in Michigan, is called the "poisoned city",[13] poisoned by its own water supply with extremely hazardous levels of lead contamination lasting for years. Residents, who are mainly black or African American and among the most impoverished of any metropolitan area in the US, are still recovering from the longterm effects of the water crisis. It is shockingly common for residents of First Nation Communities in North America to be on boil-water advisory notices and for there to be water contamination issues from polluting industries lasting years or even decades, causing rampant mercury poisoning and severe health complications.

Women are also disproportionately affected by a lack of clean drinking water, because they are often forced to spend hours fetching water every day. This was the case in Ireland for hundreds of years where it was considered a woman's role to draw and haul water from wells and springs. So constant was women's preoccupation with having to literally carry the burden of water that a parody on the traditional wedding vow "love, honour and obey" was used in an advertising slogan by a company supplying water pumps in the 1960s that read "love, honour and carry water". James Dean wrote in the *Irish Press* in 1960 why he thought this was a driver for so many women leaving the country. Since then, women worldwide remain largely excluded from water governance, despite their key role in water security.

Water for sale

An unprecedented global research collaboration between geographers, archaeologists, anthropologists, ecologists, and conservation scientists from over a dozen institutions around the world recently assessed biodiversity in relation to the history of global land use.[14] The study showed that human societies have had a deeply entwined interrelationship with Earth's ecosystems, influencing and reshaping them for at least 12,000 years. It revealed that the dramatic decline in ecosystem health and the current biodiversity crisis coincided with the rise of colonial power and industrialization leading to the unmitigated extraction, intensified land use and appropriation of Indigenous lands. One such example would be the Great Plains in what is now called New Mexico, which was once a place that was "expertly and intuitively managed between Indigenous people and bison, with grass high enough to graze a horse's belly," wrote landscape architect and environmental activist Christie Green, in 2021, in her essay *Blood Bone Oil Water*.[15] Today, the Great Plains are no longer great but are scorched bare with little or no topsoil remaining.

What do bison, grass and dirt have to do with water? The deeply rooted perennial grasses once held the soil, allowing the water to percolate, storing carbon in the deep roots. Without the rich diversity of grasses and species, water is no longer held gently, giving it time to nourish the land, but instead strips away the bare remaining crust of soil in flash floods. Water is in such short supply in the region that the Ogallala Aquifer that flows under the Great Plains is being pumped out faster than it can be replenished. Green writes about the "water for sale" signs outside farms – where farmers are selling water to oil and gas companies for fracking. This is a vicious cycle of extraction to feed another form of extraction. Water has become a commodity and is also at risk of becoming extinct.

One of the most polluting forms of extraction is mining, in which entire mountains are ripped open without a pause to consider their integral role in the water cycle. Wherever there is a mine, this disrupts the hydrology of the entire ecosystem and turns water in the earth to toxic acid, as a way of refining other harmful materials such as mercury, arsenic, lead, zinc and aluminium and all the precious metals needed for every new smartphone, laptop or car. Almost everything we consume requires some form of extraction.

A mine will continue to poison watersheds (areas of land that drain or shed water into a body of water such as a river) long after it has closed, despite Clean Water Acts being established in many countries to require mining companies to clean up. A 2,000-year-old Roman copper mine at Wadi Faynan in Jordan continues to pollute, causing degenerative diseases in living creatures, including humans. The Romans were so industrious that over the centuries of their rule they coated Greenland in 800 tons of copper and 400 tons of lead.[16] Windborne dust was carried 4,000 miles and captured in the ice crystals of falling snowflakes and imprinted layer by layer into the ice sheet.

Taming "wild" waters

What we might consider "untouched" or "wild" today has in fact had a long history interwoven with humans for millennia. What we think of as "natural" is perceived to be that way because it was sustainably managed and used by Indigenous and traditional communities to maintain or even increase the biodiversity and resilience of these systems. The science is only just beginning to catch up with the indepth ecological knowledge that Indigenous people have about the interdependence of environmental health and human health. Although the study on the history of global land use is considered groundbreaking, it simply confirms what Indigenous scientists and knowledge keepers, such as Pat McCabe, Cliff Kapono and Robin Wall Kimmerer, have always known – the importance of understanding our human connection with the rest of the living world.

We can't protect or restore the lands and the waters without the inclusion, self-determination and leadership of Indigenous communities who, although they may only exercise some level of management over five per cent of global lands, protect 80 per cent of the world's remaining biodiversity in ancestral forests, waterways, mountains and marine environments. Yet local and Indigenous voices and leaders still remain excluded from key decision-making processes seeking to reduce biodiversity loss.

The psychosocial impacts of the separation from rivers and the loss of sacred water are rarely considered, with traumatic consequences. This goes back to the idea that "we are water". As Molly Sturdevant wrote in her essay *Future Mountains* in 2021, "What's in the water is in us ... everything relies on rivers of exchange.""[17] We can feel the violence done to water in our bodies. People attach identity and belonging to rivers, especially cultural and spiritual value that can outweigh even economic concerns.

In 2021, physician and trauma expert Gabor Maté said our trauma is linked to our "power over" relationship with the Earth, and our extractive industries are a form of addiction that will destroy the planet. He argued that our disconnect from the body of the Earth mirrors the disconnect from our own bodies, which manifests, for example, in our anxieties, depression and addiction. The belief in the Earth as "something separate from us has a lot to do with patriarchal domination," he said. This feeds a reductionist response to healthcare where treatment is restricted to biological pain. Instead, "When illness comes along, it is here to teach us. The body has a message." So, too, does the water, and Maté urges us to ask, "What is the teaching?"[18]

Rivers have long been associated with powerful feminine deities, each one having its protector-goddess. We met and learned about some of these in the previous chapter. Others include Parawhenuaea, the deity for fresh water and source of the Waikato River in Aotearoa/ New Zealand, and Boann, the goddess of the River Boyne in Ireland and the source of fertility, knowledge and inspiration. The River Seine in France was named after the goddess Sequana. Europe's longest river, the Danube, gets its name from Danu, the great mother goddess who appears in both Ireland and India. The root of her name means "to flow". Anuket is the goddess of the Nile and nourisher of fields.

The Ganges is named after Ganga, goddess of purification and forgiveness, who rides a divine water creature called Makara (her *vahana* or "vehicle"). Makara are considered guardians of gateways and thresholds, emphasizing water as a portal, and can be found in the sea and freshwater. These river goddesses are typically linked to fertility and inspiration but they are also the keepers of the wisdom and power of that river. If they feel disrespected or are desecrated in any way, they have the power to violently flood the land or to withhold rain and bring drought.

This ancient association with the sacredness of water and the power of the divine feminine makes it all the more horrifying to read about the violent tactics used against women during the shocking witch trials in Europe (and later following the colonizers to the North Americas) from the 15th to the 18th centuries. It was a brutal perversion using water as a form of torture against women accused of being witches. Throughout the witch hunts in Europe, an estimated 50,000 people were executed for "witchcraft", and over 80 per cent of them were women. A preferred witch trial during the 16th century was trial by water. The accused women were tied up and thrown into a river or lake. If they floated, it was proof they were witches; if they sank, they were innocent. In either case, the end result was tragic.

Native American scholar and social activist John

Mohawk's work and writings emphasized the direct and powerful connection between the conquest and oppression of Indigenous people and other minorities (especially women) and the conquest of nature.[19] Our relationship with water today is dominated by pervasive colonial binaries that seek to sell the story that man is superior (and only certain "men" at that) to the natural world. This has violently disrupted our natural entanglement with our environment, leaving a trail of destruction.

In the context of the history of colonial slavery in the Americas, Christina Sharpe uses the term *wake* to "consider how past violence continues to resurface in the lives of African Americans today and how persistent forms of trauma and terror followed slave boats sailing across the Atlantic".[20] By that she meant that the wake or repercussions of the slave ship continue, for example, in forced movements of migrants and refugees, in the extreme racial inequalities that persist across American neighbourhoods and cities, including access to clean water and the "reappearances of the slave ship in everyday life in the form of the prison, the camp, and the school".[21]

The wake of the slave ship is felt most powerfully in the Mediterranean Sea, one of the deadliest migration routes in the world. In 2016 alone, over 5,000 people drowned trying to make the crossing. Since 2014, over 20,000 men, women and children have lost their lives trying to cross the sea in search of safety. We are all bodies of water, so the harm and oppression done to our bodies and to others is not separate from the ecological degradation and harm done to water bodies.

Restoring our relationship with water

Our water entanglements – that ecological way of being, our interdependence with the vitality of water – have been "bulldozed over by modernity", to quote Irish author Emma Dabiri.[22] To restore our relationship with water we need to reawaken new and alternative forms of consciousness that reclaim a place-based understanding of how we relate to our water systems in a way that challenges the destructive forces of colonization. This is "power with", not "power over".

Blue ecology, the concept that interweaves First Nations and Western thought and developed by Michael Blackstock and other Indigenous scholars mentioned in Chapter 1, is one way that recognizes the shared bond we have with water and the central role that the life spirit of water plays in not only generating and sustaining life but also unifying life. The essence of blue ecology is interconnectedness, a fluid, cyclical flow that is nonexistent within dominant systems of capitalism and colonialism.

Restoring our rivers and wetlands is key to how well we will be able to adapt to the changes already underway. Rivers are part of an intricate system of interdependence, providing multiple ecological benefits that no amount of geoengineering could match – a system where there is a remarkable symbiosis and complex interplay between plants, trees, land-based creatures, fish, plankton, water and the ocean.

It may seem obvious that salmon are good for rivers, an indicator of a healthy river system, but they are also good for the forests. In the region of the Pacific North West, where there are still some remaining old-growth forest, with bears and wild salmon river runs, scientists have discovered huge quantities of nitrogen in the trees alongside salmon rivers. This type of nitrogen, isotope nitrogen-15, comes from the ocean and is present in as much as 70 per cent of the plants growing along these rivers. Bears, as they hunt and gorge on salmon, begin to get selective, eating the high-energy parts of salmon, such as the caviar (eggs), and discarding the rest for other animals to scavenge. These salmon remains are full of nitrogen that helps to fertilize the soil and can be carried further through animal faeces into the woods lining the waterways.

In turn, trees are good for the ocean. As a young college student studying botany and biochemistry, Irish scientist Diana Beresford-Kroeger noticed, while out scouting for plant specimens on the south coast of Ireland, that the rarest plants were often found where freshwater mixed with saltwater, where rivers met the sea. She believed that the freshwater must be carrying a rare mineral from the land into the sea that encouraged this diversity and profusion of rare plant species. About half a century later she met Japanese marine chemist Katsuhiko Matsunaga, who confirmed her hunch.[23]

After decades of research, spurred by the worrying collapse of coastal marine ecosystems in Japan, Matsunaga and his team proved the connection between trees and the sea. Rich leaf litter contains acids that leach into the ground and bond with iron in the soil, boosting the growth of plankton, the basis of the food chain. More trees means more fish in the sea. However, the flipside is all too true, as clear-cutting forests depletes coastal ecosystems, starving marine life and leading to ecosystem collapse.

Trees also increase humidity exchange, swelling local rainfall. A tree with a 20m (65½ft) diameter will breathe (circulate and release) an average of 1,000 litres (1,760 pints) of water a day. One key way to restore the health of woodland ecosystems, river systems and coastal habitats is to replant native woodland where it has been lost in coastal areas and along waterways. Core samples taken from ancient tree fragments that still remain in old-growth forest in parts of British Columbia reveal how much more plentiful the salmon who once swam in the rivers were, coinciding with the greatest periods of growth for the trees. The narrowing between the trees' growth rings mirrors the dramatic decline of salmon in the last one hundred years, and in many places the isotope nitrogen-15 can no longer be detected in the trees. The ocean has vanished from the woods.

There are a growing number of successful campaigns led by river guardians and water protectors all over the world to free the rivers. In Salt Lake City, long-buried rivers have recently been brought to light. For decades the three major creeks running from the Wasatch Mountains into the Jordan River have been forced underground into manmade tunnels, artificially channelling the water rather than allowing it to meander and merge. A nonprofit environmental group has now uncovered the confluence, and a neglected urban space has been replaced by the Three Creeks Confluence Park: a slick, modern echoing of the ancient reverence that has always been shown to the mixing of waters.

Arteries can be unblocked. With proper care, social changes and in some cases major restoration work, the lifeblood of the planet can flow freely again. In 2016, the largest dam removal project in the United States was completed. The Elwha River in Washington State saw the successful return of salmon species in a matter of years, and crucially the return of the river delta and sediment and nutrients supporting critical nursery habitats such as eel grass beds, which also act as important carbon sinks, absorbing carbon from the atmosphere and keeping it stored in the seabed. This was followed by the agreement to begin the removal of four dams on the Klamath River in California after decades of advocacy by the Yurok tribe and other river defenders who formed the Klamath Justice Coalition.[24] It will be the largest dam removal project in US history. One of the campaigners, Annelia Hillman, described the river as "our umbilical cord".[25]

Restoring the balance of power

Restoration can help us enter a relationship once again with the more-than-human world, but only if we consider how and why we value the water or land. Indigenous botanist Robin Wall Kimmerer argued in 2015 that we must first ask what water means to us. Is it another resource or commodity or is it our life force and spiritual home? "Restoring land for production of natural resources," she said, "is not the same as renewal of land for cultural identity."[26]

If we approach restoration with the same mechanistic view of dominion, where an ecosystem is a machine rather than a community of sovereign beings, then we are destined to fail. If we can follow Kimmerer's call for a covenant of reciprocity,[27] there is hope for recovery. One way to do this is the granting of legal personhood to rivers, a powerful example of "power to", giving back agency and sovereignty to the water.

The dam removal project on the Klamath was preceded by the granting of legal personhood to the river by the Yurok tribe, while the Arato in Columbia was the first river to be a legal person under the Rights of Nature framework in 2016. Since then, there have been many more examples, including the Whanganui River in Aotearoa/New Zealand and the Ganges in India in 2017.

A universal declaration on the rights of rivers has also been established, asserting that all rivers possess fundamental rights, including: *the right to flow, the right to perform essential functions within its ecosystem, the right to be free from pollution, the right to feed and be fed by sustainable aquifers, the right to native biodiversity, and the right to regeneration and restoration.*[28]

Momentum is growing for a World Water Law,[29] to build on the dedication of water guardians around the world who have committed their lives to the protection and reverence of water on behalf of all life. This law would align human law with the original laws of life/nature, uniting people around our shared water bond and demand an internationally binding law for the protection of water.

In 2019, legal scholar Kelsey Leonard, from the Shinnecock Nation, explained in a powerful TED talk why granting lakes and rivers legal "personhood" – giving them the same legal rights as humans – is the first step to protecting our bodies of water and fundamentally transforming how we value this vital resource. "I was taught that water is alive," Leonard said. "It can hear; it holds memories. And so I brought a water vessel up with me today because I want it to hold the memories of our conversation today."[30]

Leonard argued that we need to change the way we value water, and in particular to think about how we connect to water, and that granting water legal personhood status would address these water injustices. She likened it to granting legal personhood to other nonhuman entities such as corporations. "I believe that one of the many solutions to solving the many water injustices we see in our world today," she continued, "is recognizing that water is a living relation and granting it the legal personhood it deserves."

This is not something new. Indigenous legal systems have already set a precedent for this, based on the foundational principle of "understanding nonhuman relations as being living and protected under our laws", and have holistic management approaches to water systems.

River guardians and waterkeepers

The granting of legal personhood and river rights requires the rivers to have someone to speak on their behalf – this is "power with". Who are the people that listen to and speak for the waters?

Maida Bilal and a group of local women are defenders of one of Europe's last wild rivers, the Kruščica in Bosnia and Herzegovina. In 2021, Bilal received the renowned Goldman Environmental Prize, the so-called Green Nobel Prize, on behalf of the women who protected the river from a damming project that was proceeding without following any proper legal consultation with local communities.[31] The women occupied the bridge over the river during a long cold winter for over 500 days and nights, despite violent attempts by the police to evict them, and prevented the construction of two hydropower plants. They took the case to court and won on the grounds that hydropower poses one of the greatest threats to wild rivers and to the people who live along them. "We are the corrective force," said Bilal. "We are the guardians of this land." The bridge has become known as the "Brave Women of Kruščica" bridge.

This campaign is part of a wider coalition in the Balkans region, where 80 per cent of rivers remain very healthy (as opposed to the rest of Europe), called Save the Blue Heart of Europe. Thirty-eight hydropower dams are proposed on the 270km-long (168 miles) Vjosa River and its tributaries, which is the last free-flowing, undammed river system in Europe. The campaign has gained huge international attention, resulting in several European banks pulling their funding for hydropower projects, and the committee of the Bern Convention, one of the most important nature conservation agreements in Europe, to target "crimes against nature" in the region.

The world needs healthy rivers, and lower-impact energy options exist beyond hydropower. We need to consider low cost "green infrastructure" alternatives such as proper habitat restoration and water conservation measures that have proven to be far more effective at protecting water supply and mitigating the risks of climate change.

Water protector Pat McCabe believes we have a commitment to Earth and the capacity to help her and the rest of life thrive, a refreshing, alternative and uplifting view to the dominant narrative that humans are the source of all the ills and suffering of the world. McCabe believes that it should matter to all of us how Indigenous cultures, the people who hold the really deep science of sustainability and regeneration, are doing. At the core of these practices is listening – creating a society that cultivates practices that enables us to listen. What would the water say to us if we understood how to listen to it? "How do we recognize that we belong to Earth, to water, and water doesn't belong to us?" she asked me.

McCabe told me about an agricultural water system called "acequia", where she lives in northern New Mexico. Water comes down off the mountain into the valley and is channelled by irrigation ditches that carry the water like arteries. Each ditch has a name and has been maintained for hundreds if not thousands of years, connecting people closely to the importance of the flow of water for giving life. She explained it was likely established by the Red Willow people who have lived there for at least 3,000 years. A long lineage of people maintain the flow of these water arteries to irrigate the land, with every person responsible for keeping their ditch clear so that the water can flow on to their neighbours' land, and so on.

What is common to all of these victories for restoring rights to rivers, reclaiming the free-flowing power of water, is the importance of community and coalition building. One such example is Friends of Lake

Turkana, a cooperative movement founded by Kenyan environmentalist Ikal Angelei to halt the development of a hydroelectric dam that would block access to the water for Indigenous communities around the lake and have widespread environmental and cultural implications. UNESCO ruled in favour of the Friends of Lake Turkana, and Angelei was awarded the Goldman Prize in 2012. The non-government organization (NGO) People and Water, which was founded by hydrologist Michal Kravčík, is another example of a model of river guardianship based on democratic, local communities taking ownership over water management and governance.

The rapidly growing Waterkeeper Alliance is a global movement to protect water resources, currently uniting more than 350 waterkeeper organizations and affiliates throughout over 47 countries in the Americas, Europe, Australia, Asia and Africa. One of these projects is the Waiwai Ola Waterkeepers of the Hawaiian islands headed up by Rhiannon "Rae" Tereari'i Chandler-'Iao. Rae explained, "Waterkeepers work to protect the ability of present and future generations to swim, fish, drink, and otherwise use and enjoy the waters that support the people and culture of Hawai'i."[32]

For the waterkeepers of the Xakriaba tribe from the São Francisco river basin in northeast Brazil, the river is not limited to a location on a map but carries the stories and legends of the place and sustains their identity. Campaigning for access to the river is not enough, as this is also about the ability to care for it. In a moving tribute to the life force of the river, a group of Xakriaba activists recorded a song. In the video, they stand up to their waists in the flow of the waters and sing "We are the rivers. . ."

EXERCISE:
JOURNALING AND REFLECTING

When I go down to the water, I draw on its surface the shape of a wolf that has been gone from this land for 300 years, along with ancient oak woodlands and free-flowing riparian systems. I am inspired to do this after reading Jaime Luis Huenún's powerful poem about helping the free water defend itself by drawing a tiger on the stream.[33]

Journaling prompts

If you are thinking of journaling about water, here are some prompts that may help you:

- As water scientist Dr Kelsey Leonard reminds us, ask yourself each day, "What have I done for the water today?"
- What would you draw with your finger on the surface of the water to set it free once again?
- Consider: What is a river? Write, draw, sing or dance whatever comes up in response to this question.

A practice for water reciprocity

Before entering the water, especially for your own benefit to bathe, swim, play or take water to drink, you can follow these five steps to improve the feeling of connection between your body and the water.

1. First sense and observe the energy of the river, lake, sea or surf before rushing out there.
2. Acknowledge the water by name and share why you have come.
3. Deepen and slow your breath, extending your exhale to release any tension in your body, allowing yourself to become soft, more like water.
4. Seek the blessing of the water in whichever form feels good. I always first sprinkle the water on my forehead, almost like receiving a sacrament but also helping to attune my physical body to the qualities of the water that day.
5. You may wish to make a small offering (seashells or pebbles arranged and left on the tideline, for example) or offer prayer or song to the water before you leave.

CHAPTER 6

RISING

Climate change is the story of water and its transformation from one state to another (such as permafrost to water to vapour) and its dramatic movement from one place to another (such as glaciers to rivers to oceans to clouds). As I wrote these words, one of Antarctica's most important ice shelves that holds back the so-called Doomsday Glacier is "shattering like broken glass" and dissolving into the Great Southern Ocean. The change is rapid; a process that should take geologic time, the time it takes rocks to form, is happening in our lifetime. Within 10 to 20 years, if fossil-fuel-driven warming continues (and maybe it is already irreversible), the ice sheet will be gone forever. There is no restoring or returning the ice to its solid state once it has melted, and no geoengineering will save us.

In 2019, the UN Intergovernmental Panel on Climate Change (IPCC) published its "Special Report on the Ocean and the Cryosphere in a Changing World", clearly outlining that we are the last generation able to save the Earth from irreversible destruction.[1] It became obvious from the report that the future of our planet is going to become a lot more oceanic. Perhaps this is the greatest demonstration of planetary interconnectedness, linking what is happening at the distant poles of the Earth with the local, lived realities of rising seas everywhere.

Rising sea levels

On my drive home one evening, a climate scientist from the University College Dublin was giving a brief talk on the afterwork radio show about the catastrophe unfolding in Antarctica. She explained that this will create a 65cm (25½in), or 25 per cent, increase in global sea level rise within 10 to 20 years. Until recently, most forecasts had predicted a 65cm sea level rise by 2100, not by 2030 or 2040. The climate scientist said that this changes everything.

"Ice has memory," Robert Macfarlane wrote in *Underland*.[2] The memory of ice extends back over a million years, recording every little detail of Earth's history in its core. Ice stores the chemical composition of the air – the days of sunshine, precipitation, volcanic eruptions, mining waste, bombs and greenhouse gas emissions. It may seem solid and inert, with the polar regions remaining a frozen wasteland for all eternity, but Macfarlane reminded us that it is now becoming a lively substance. He explained how the language of ice is also changing, with the terms "glacial pace" and "permafrost" (to be permanently frozen) losing their meaning.

Change is happening so fast that it is impossible for cartographers to keep up with the mapping of where the ice meets the sea. The ice edge has become so fluid and transient that it can no longer be drawn as a single line. These places of ice now feel the thinnest, like the "thin places" common in Celtic tradition, where the boundaries or borders between worlds lie, where the time between this place and some other place yet to be born or realized is most fragile. These are like crumbling edge-spaces, the borders between solid ice and sea, between the buried chemical weapons and waste of World War II and our children's future.

Washing away the past

It is not only ice that we thought could hold our secrets forever – the sea, too, has been used to erase our past. Australian feminist scholar Astrida Neimanis investigates the consequence of the dominant perception of the ocean as being "unfathomable", a place to disappear our unwanted terrestrial things and a place of forgetting, where the purpose of the sea is the "washing away [of] human sins".[3] She explores the dumping of unused World War II chemical weapons, mostly mustard gas, in Gotland Deep in the Baltic Sea. Estimates vary widely from 2,000 to 10,000 tons and the exact locations of the toxic waste remains unknown, at least until these forgotten chemical weapons resurface three-quarters of a century later, burning the skin from seals and killing unsuspecting fishermen who haul the waste caught in their nets aboard their boats. Neimanis writes in *Blue Legalities* that the sea is also "a well of remembrance".[4]

In the 1950s, marine biologist and writer Rachel Carson recognized how the boundaries between sea and land are fleeting and transitory. At the time, she wrote about the ebb and flow of the sea on a grand scale: the great floods of prehistory during the Cretaceous era 60 million to 130 million years ago, when half of Europe and North America were submerged, and the fall of sea levels during the last ice age. This is the first time in human history that these boundaries have been in such a state of flux.

Sixty-five centimetres (25½in) may not seem like much but even in Ireland we are already experiencing the impacts of increasingly more extreme storms, flooding and coastal erosion. The wetlands would be the first to go; those fragile, biodiverse, species-rich liminal spaces. My beloved Durnesh Lagoon, a drowned memory, would be land reclaimed by the sea once again. Maybe in an era of leavetakings, it is no longer useful to dream the Earth undrowned, as Elizabeth Rush proclaimed in her book *Rising*.

With the birth of Ireland as an independent free state in 1922, as capitalism replaced colonialism, nature was woven into a zeal to "modernize". Irish journalist Fintan O'Toole argued in the *Irish Times*, in 2021, that this rampant "environmental vandalism" is evident in our most abundant resource: water.[5] Nearly half of surface waters in Ireland are failing to meet the legally binding water quality objectives set by the EU Water Framework Directive, and the decline is accelerating rapidly. Before 2015, the Environmental Protection Agency (EPA) stated that only 1.4 per cent of Irish rivers had evidence of increasing levels of pollutants, primarily nitrates. However, the EPA's 2020 report stated that almost half of all rivers are becoming increasingly polluted with these chemicals.[6]

In a period of less than 20 years we lost 258,800 hectares of marine wetlands. Protected status seems meaningless when only 15 per cent of habitats protected under EU law have a "favourable" status and almost half are in continuing decline. The loss of wetlands means the loss of species that depend on them. Waders such as the curlew, lapwing, dunlin and redshank have suffered a 93 per cent decline in breeding populations.

"This fecklessness," O'Toole wrote, "might most charitably be interpreted as a postcolonial hangover. It is as if the land and everything in it still belongs to somebody else."

The questions might be: Do we love a place enough to care for it? And is it too late to undo the damage?

Disappearing waves

I think back to the climate scientist speaking on the radio about the rise in global sea level and wonder about the waves I love to surf. Maybe that seems an absurd concern to have when the entire Netherlands is less than 65cm (25½in) above sea level, and when Bangladesh, Maldives, Micronesia, Palau, Amsterdam, Chennai, Los Angeles and Miami would be under water too. But if the waves I love to surf disappeared, the very interaction between ocean waves and the seabed, the coral reefs, rocky shores and sandy coasts would be altered forever. There would be no natural barriers to slow the power of those waves as they came crashing higher and higher onto the land.

Mangroves, salt marshes, kelp forests, coral reefs, sand bars and sand dunes would disappear, no longer able to slow the waves' landward march. Reliant on light for photosynthesis, kelp forests survive best in shallow open waters along rocky coastlines with cool temperatures and would not have time to migrate to shallower water. We would be left completely exposed, naked, to the raw intensity of an ocean striking back. What does blue health and blue space mean when that happens? Will surfing be found only in artificial wave pools or manmade water installations in chemically "purified", lifeless water, for the privileged few to enjoy?

Throughout history, powerful individual waves that seem to possess otherworldly forces have been given recognition in the memory of people. In Ireland, these great ocean waves have been given names such as Tonn Tuaithe and Tonn Rudhraige. Irish documentary-maker Manchán Magan writes in *Thirty-two Words for Field* how ocean waves "thunder around the island's perimeter, protecting the land, binding and controlling existence, much like a particle or gravitational forces".[7] It is thought that the stories of these waves passed down through time may have their origins in the ancestral memory of ancient geological events associated with the end of the last ice age, when glacial floods of water gushed from the land and poured out of the rivers and into the sea, creating huge surging waves.

I wonder if any other radio listeners were imagining what 65cm (25½in) of sea level rise meant for their home or places of belonging? Were their eyes watering with tears too? The scientist reminded the listeners that this is only what is happening in Antarctica; it did not account for the Greenland ice sheet, the already rapidly melting Arctic and global glaciers. In the last two decades, according to Danish climate researchers, the volume of ice-melt in Greenland would be enough to flood the entire United States in 0.5m (20in) of water. This extensive loss of ice has already contributed to 1.2cm (½in) of global sea-level rise in just 20 years. In terms of direct human impact, for every centimetre rise in global sea level, according to climate scientist Professor Andrew Shepherd at the University of Leeds in London, another six million people are exposed to coastal flooding.[8]

Impact on the ocean

What the climate scientist on the radio did not have time to mention is what all that freshwater will do to the salinity of the sea in one of the greatest hotspots for biodiversity on the planet. Are we witnessing the end of the oceans?, as claimed by the Australian culture and politics magazine *The Monthly* in 2018.[9]

Whales migrate to feed in the krill-rich waters surrounding the poles, dependent on the finely balanced chemistry of the ocean. The Great Southern Ocean is one of the most important feeding grounds for a whole cascade of marine life from zooplankton to blue whales. The excessive flood of meltwater gushing into the waters around Greenland in the Arctic is already reducing ocean salinity, slowing the reproduction rate of zooplankton, the building blocks of the entire oceanic food web. Zooplankton are the main diet of krill, which are the primary food source of whale species such as the humpback. Krill populations have fallen by 80 per cent since the 1970s, failing to reproduce in more acidic waters.

Although many species of whales are showing remarkable signs of recovery, new research shows that pre-whaling populations were hugely underestimated. Through genetic testing, scientists can now prove there may have been six times the numbers of humpback whales in the world. Various populations of humpback whales have made a striking recovery in important breeding and birthing waters such as the Hawaiian islands, where they numbered some 800 individuals in 1979. Today there are more than 10,000. But for whales, their future as much as ours is tied to an ocean under stress from chemical, sonic, ecological and meteorological pressures that are altering its makeup and functioning.

The impact of all this is, in part, believed to be contributing to the near extinction of wild Atlantic salmon, a creature that has shaped my ancestry, providing the first people to arrive in Ireland with the energy and nutrition they needed to thrive. Salmon were once so plentiful that the journals of Captain Meriwether Lewis and Lieutenant William Clark from their 1805 expedition along the Columbia River in the United States reported that it was possible to walk across the fish's backs to cross the river.[10] Similar accounts exist in Ireland regarding the Atlantic salmon. What will it mean when the last wild Atlantic salmon becomes a keening lament? As we explored in the previous chapter, the loss of wonder and awe that a living, animate ocean instils will alter our relationship with the depths of our psyche when we encounter an ocean that is tainted, silent and seething with fury.

A breathless ocean

How might we shift from a landcentric view to a watercentric view on this blue planet? And how would that help us with the mess we are in? If we had an oceancentric view, our response to the climate crisis and the solutions we need would be very different.

Holly Jean Buck, US professor of the environment and sustainability, speaks about the absence of the ocean in climate mitigation interventions, with our fixation on landbased metrics of temperature and precipitation, and sea-level rise from the point of view of how it encroaches on us and our land. If we were ocean dwellers, she wrote in the book *Blue Legalities*, "our working groups and panels might be studying different triple threats: ocean acidification, ocean warming and deoxygenization."[11]

Without the ocean, the average global temperature would already be more than double – 50°C (122°F) instead of the current 15°C (59°F) – and we would be toast. This is because the ocean absorbs excess heat – according to the International Union for Conservation of Nature (IUCN), it has absorbed 93 per cent of heat trapped by greenhouse gases since the 1970s.[12] The ocean also regulates what water researcher Theodor Schwenk refers to as the Earth's great respiratory processes, including the water cycle.

Water in the air drives all of Earth's weather processes. Seasonal shifts in temperature between landmasses and the world's seas cause the air to rise over warmer continents in summer and fall over cooler seas. In winter the pattern is reversed. In this way, the Earth breathes itself, circulating water around the planet. Unfortunately, climate change is intensifying the global water cycle. The latest evidence shows that every aspect of the Earth's water cycle has intensified at twice the predicted rate, taking more freshwater away from equatorial regions, accelerating drought and pushing more water to the poles, intensifying flooding.

This change in the Earth's circulatory and respiratory systems is wreaking havoc on water security. Around 1.1 billion people worldwide lack access to water, and a total of 2.7 billion find water scarce for at least one month of the year.[13] According to International Rivers, in 2019 nearly 25 per cent of the world's population faced severe water scarcity. By 2050, researchers predict that up to half the world's population will live in water-stressed areas.[14] It is also estimated that by 2030 up to 700 million people could be displaced worldwide due to water scarcity, at a time when global demand for water continues to grow. According to the Organisation for Economic Co-operation and Development (OECD), most of that increase is occurring as a result of growing demand from industry, which includes energy generation.

The ability of the ocean to breathe for the planet, to exhale oxygen (from phytoplankton, sea grasses, seaweeds and mangroves) and to inhale carbon dioxide by taking its surplus from the atmosphere to maintain a balance that promotes life on Earth, has been gravely compromised. The ocean has absorbed such an excess of carbon dioxide, about a quarter of the carbon pollution created each year by burning fossil fuels, that it is beginning to suffocate. This increase in carbon dioxide has altered the ocean's pH, causing widespread acidification and dissolving the building blocks of life. Humanity is changing the composition of the atmosphere and the ocean.

"Ocean acidification" was the term coined in 2003 by atmospheric scientist Ken Caldeira, but the concept has largely passed us by even though it is one of the most significant changes in our planet's chemistry and constitution over the last 30 million to 50 million years. Perhaps this is because new words take time to have meaning.

"How do we communicate," Icelandic writer and activist Andri Snaer Magnason asked in *On Time and Water*, "the sensations that arise from a knowledge of the impending death of everything (we) love(d)?" Words affect our emotions, our feelings, and "words have different charges to them," he wrote, with new concepts taking many years "to reach full charge".[15]

Ocean acidification is making it tougher for shellfish and coral to survive. Half of the Great Barrier Reef's corals have died in the last 25 years due to these global changes in the ocean's chemistry, causing mass coral bleaching events. As oceans become more acidic, it makes it harder for shellfish and other species to build shells and may impact the nervous systems of sharks, clownfish and other marine life.

New York professor of environment and sustainability Holly Jean Buck explained in *Blue Legalities* that the surface ocean water before increased industrialization was weakly alkaline, with a pH of 8.2. Its fall to 8.1 today seems deceptively minimal, but, as Buck explained, "pH is measured on a logarithmic scale – this drop corresponds to an increase in surface ocean acidity by 26 per cent."[16]

The United Nations predicts that by the end of the century, the kaleidoscopic vibrant coral reefs of the world, home to the richest biodiversity of life on Earth, could be lost. How will I explain the loss of this thriving, humming magical underwater world that I had the privilege to experience in the early 2000s to my children? Diving at night with phytoplankton, zooplankton and dinoflagellates lighting up underwater like a colourful neon metropolis, and during the day almost bumping into sea turtles, hovering above manta rays as they somersaulted below me and dodging the dive-bombing of huge flocks of frigate birds.

The vulnerability of watersheds

Each of us lives within a watershed (also called a drainage basin or catchment area). A watershed is an area of land where all the rainfall collects and flows or drains into the same place – a river, lake or sea. A small watershed may be the drainage area for a local stream or creek. The largest watershed in the world is the Amazon River basin, which is made up of many smaller watersheds all coming together. Interestingly we use the term "watershed moment" to define a turning point in our lives, like the dividing rises between mountains that send the water flowing down either side in different directions.

Through a deepening of our understanding of watersheds we can come together as a community to help restore our waters. Hawaiian culture may hold a long-overdue solution to the pollution problem, the *ahupua'a* system, which recognizes that we all live downstream. This means that we all have personal responsibility for the part of the watershed we are connected to, from *uka* (uplands), *kula* (midlands) to *kai* (ocean).

This is more than a resource management system. "Where we are determines how we behave," explained Hawaii cultural ambassador Kainoa Horcajo in the 2019 documentary *Wai Wai*. In the summit area, he said, "it is the realm of the gods, it's like being in church. . . we step with reverence."[17]

Where water first touches the islands in the mountains, it is considered sacred and pure. In ancient Irish culture, the place between the mountain and the sky was considered to be one of three sacred spaces because it was where water met land. The other sacred spaces were where rock meets sea and where the bark of a tree meets the cambium, or living layer, of a tree, which is also responsible for the transport of water from the roots to the leaves. As surfer-scientist Cliff Kapono explained in Chapter 2, each element and form of water is a physical manifestation of the gods. The rain clouds correlate with Lono, the god of agriculture, and when rain falls from the clouds onto the land it becomes Kane, associated with moving freshwater. This is where we, as humanity, meet the water and interact with it in our daily lives.

Waikiki, the famous stretch of coast in the city of Honolulu that attracts millions of tourists to its artificially made beaches and hotel resorts every year, was once a vast drainage basin of wetland and marshland ecosystems that gathered and purified the water before it flowed into the sea. The name "Wai ki ki" means spouting water, a spring-fed place. In the Waikiki watershed, the flow of water was carefully managed to grow taro and create fish ponds for over a thousand years, always ensuring the flow of water was maintained downstream. This system based on the water cycle is called the *ahupua'a*, "*mauka to makai*", or mountain to ocean, watershed management approach.

Cliff Kapono explained to me that if the flow of water has been manipulated for irrigating taro, the water must be returned to its original path for the benefit of all life downstream. "We knew the destruction caused by disrupting the flow of water from Kane (the god of the flowing freshwater) to Kanaloa (the god of saltwater), you remove the balance," he said. Kapono described the water cycle as a series of interconnected familial relationships made animate and represented by various deities and gods, and added that the role of the goddesses is to help mediate the flow and maintain the balance of the water cycle. The disruption of this flow causes a lot of "family" issues among the various representatives of water.

"The goddesses are seen as very integral in the meeting between the waters," he said. "They act as water bearers." He recited their names, embodying the altered states of water: "Poliahu is the snow, Lilinoe, the soft mist, and there's percolating water, and all these different forms and ways water moves and is transferred."

The widespread diversion and extraction of water for industrial sugar cane plantations (and more recently mass-scale tourism) caused severe downstream water shortages and some watersheds to dry up completely, a problem that is ongoing in the Hawaiian islands. Not allowing water to percolate into the earth and replenish aquifers has led to a drop in the water table. With sea levels rising, there is the real potential that the islands' drinking water may become more salt than fresh. Kapono explained to me that the "surf paradise" of Waikiki is sinking. Today there are no wetlands to filter the storm waters after heavy rains, leading to the pollution of coastal waters, while tens of thousands of tons of sand have to be transported to Waikiki, as flooding from high tides and storm surges that strip the coast bare have become more frequent.

The waterkeeper movement is working to redress some of these imbalances. Hawaiian waterkeeper, Rae, shared that each family typically has a protector or *amakua* that is connected to water. She is using innovative nature-based solutions to address local water quality challenges. Reintroducing the black lipped pearl oyster and other native oysters helps to clean up and care for nearshore waters such as Pearl Harbor and Waikiki, which has been negatively affected by land-use changes. Increasing the oyster population helps to clean the waters entering popular swimming and surfing areas, combined with ongoing community-based monitoring of the health of watersheds.

Almost all parts of the world are experiencing imbalances in the water cycle caused by climate change. In some places, the consequences are felt much more severely, as hundreds of millions of people rely on seasonal glacial meltwater for their fresh water supply. For example, the 300,000 people living in Ladakh Valley, an arid, high mountain region of northern India in the rain shadow of the Himalayas, are almost entirely dependent on glacial meltwater for drinking and to irrigate crops.

The shrinking and disappearance of glaciers means these meltwaters are arriving later and later every year, leading to crop failure. To find a short-term solution to this crisis, Indian engineer Sonam Wangchuk invented the "ice stupas",[18] which tower 30–50m (98½–164ft) and are semi-sculptural, yet entirely practical structures of ice shaped like the high, narrow domes of Buddhist stupas. The ice stupas' design slows the melting of the ice and can provide millions of litres of water for each community to use, extending the growing season, until the glacial meltwater flows again later in the summer.

We need both science and Indigenous wisdom, says Chadian environmental activist Hindou Oumarou Ibrahim.[19] In her TED talk, she shares how her nomadic community who live on the shores of the shrinking Lake Chad is working closely with scientists to restore endangered ecosystems, offering lessons on how to create more resilient communities. Ibrahim uses 3D participatory mapping to show the traditional ecological knowledge of place, combined with scientific datasets from climate and meteorological scientists. Women's knowledge is essential, integrating detailed information about the locations of food species and medicinal plants and access to water, helping to monitor, manage and restore ecosystems.

Ibrahim advocates for the integration and honouring of Indigenous knowledge in our response to water and climate crises. Indigenous knowledge has been developed over millennia, whereas western science was developed in the last 200 years in response to colonial and capitalist agendas. "Science is how capitalism knows the world," wrote activist Rebecca Solnit in 2016.[20]

A series of images in Dark Mountain's *Abyss* issue shows a block of ice made from river water, carved like an open book, resting between the rocks in a shallow, fast-moving stream. Held within the melting ice are seeds belonging to mountain maple, columbine flower, blue spruce and other native flora. Basia Irland's project "Receding/Reseeding"[21] combines the communal effort and local and scientific knowledge to address complex issues of climate disruption, receding glaciers, poisonous discharge from mines and watershed restoration by releasing these seed-impregnated ice sculptures into rivers. By carving the ice into the shape of an open or closed book, embedded with seeds, Irland is creating a new ecological language of place. Her "ice books" have been created around the world and released on river restoration walks with local communities and scientists to bring attention to the high level of pollution in rivers and streams. Irland's project highlights how the water crisis we face is a crisis of broken relationships, and that one way to restore these relationships is through storytelling.

Water walks

The connection between women, water activism and restoration is strong. More often than not, it is women who are standing on the frontlines of water protection for their communities. One way women have raised awareness of the need to restore our waters is by organizing water walks. The Great Earth Water Walk, initiated in 2003 and continuing to 2017, was led by water protectors and Indigenous elders such as Josephine Mandamin when they and their supporters walked around the shoreline of each of the Great Lakes, culminating in a walk up the St Lawrence River to where it meets the Atlantic Ocean. The intention was not only to raise awareness but to give all participants a deeper form of engagement with each of the Great Lakes.

After the experience, Mandamin shared how she came to understand that each lake has its own distinct qualities and messages to communicate. For example, how Lake Huron demonstrated "the gelling together as male and female", while Lake Erie demonstrated to the walkers "how people can be dead to themselves".[22] Around the nuclear power plants of Lake Ontario there was a feeling of heaviness, which Mandamin described in this way: "None of us touched that water for some reason because we felt it was so polluted. . . We were afraid to; there was something in the water we were afraid of."

The Great Earth Water Walks around the lakes inspired others to initiate water walks along the rivers, lakes or water bodies where they lived. Maria, another water walker, realized that even though we may live by a river we know very little about it: how it is doing, how damaged it is, what makes its home there and what grows there.

As well as acts of reconnection and active engagement, water walks are forms of protest. In 2013, a three-day 100km (62-mile) ceremonial water walk protested about the spilling of 1.6 million litres of bitumen at Cold Lake at Alberta, Canada.[23] Canadian Poet Rita Wong reflected on the Healing Walk in the Tar Sands in the article "Ethical Waters".[24] This walk was a somewhat terrifying loop around the middle of the Alberta oil industry's ground zero, where richly forested lands have been turned inside out, trees and topsoil eviscerated from the landscape, and oil replaces water; for every barrel of oil, the equivalent of three to four barrels of water are polluted.

Wong drew stark parallels with the Memorial March for Missing and Murdered Women, which Albertan environmental activist Cleo Reece helped to initiate. Reece spoke of the connection between the violence against Indigenous women and the violence against Indigenous watersheds. "Colonisation is not a thing of the past," she said in Wong's article. "It continues today in virulent, violent forms, in both the slow poisoning of water and the fast killing of women."

Rise: from one island to another

At the end of the recordbreaking hot summer of 2018, two women stood on a melting glacier. Kathy Jetñil-Kijiner, Marshallese poet and climate activist, and Inuk writer and climate activist Aka Niviâna were shouting a poem above the groaning of the glacier, roar of wind and thundering meltwater. They were on the south coast of Kalaalilit Nunaat (meaning the Land of the People), or Greenland – the biggest island on Earth. One is a sister of ice and snow; the other is a sister of ocean and sand from far, far away in the South Pacific's Marshall Islands. Despite the distance between their homelands, they are connected from one island to another through the interdependence of water and ice.

Science and reason alone have not and will not solve this climate crisis. The facts and figures have failed to move us, but there is great power in poetry that speaks to our emotions and intuition, allowing us to feel and igniting a spark in our bellies. Jetñil-Kijiner and Niviâna created their collaborative poem, "Rise", to show how these two islands are affected by climate change and how the melting glaciers will contribute to rising sea levels.

The performance of the poem was at a ceremony called "Rise: From One Island to Another" – the acknowledging of each other's homeland and heritage with the offering of gifts: a shell from the land of ocean, and sand and rocks from the land of snow and ice. Before they met for the first time, the women worked together for weeks, agreeing that they should make the poem a conversation and include a myth or an oral story from their Indigenous cultures. The myths they drew upon warn of the dangers of disrespecting the power of the water, sea and land.

Jetñil-Kijiner began the poem with the myth of two sisters turned to stone "rooted to the reef forever".[25] Niviâna drew on the story of Sassuma Arnaa, Mother of the Sea (also known as Sedna), which is told to every Greenlandic child – to respect the land and sea. The ice, streams and whales are all Sassuma Arnaa's children. "She sees the greed in our hearts, the disrespect in our eyes," Niviâna intoned. There is a stunning life-size monument carved in the goddess's honour at the old harbour in Nuuk. Sassuma Arnaa rests in a tidal rockpool by the sea with the waves crashing around her, seated on her oceanic throne surrounded by creatures from the sea – polar bear, walrus, seal, salmon and whale – and a young man seeking either her blessing or forgiveness at her feet.

Jetñil-Kijiner spoke about "the lagoon that will devour you", in reference to the rising sea levels that are threatening the Marshall Islands, which will be one of the first regions to disappear, caused by the melting of the very ice the women stand upon. She founded Jo-Jikum to teach the Marshallese youth about environmental issues and give them space to voice their opinions on what they want for their country and how to get involved in the community.

In the poem, the women recognize the shared trauma inflicted on their islands by others, both impacted by the brutal outcomes from wars not of their making. The Bikini Atoll was blasted by US nuclear testing during the Cold War in 1954 by a bomb that was 1,000 times more powerful than the atomic bomb dropped on Hiroshima. The bomb shattered the coral reef, creating a mile-wide crater and leaving a violent legacy of land and water contamination, environmental degradation and reproductive toxicity for generations, and a people who remain displaced from their ancestral lands to this day.

In another poem by Jetñil-Kijiner, called "Monster", she wrote about the devastating and violent legacy caused by the nuclear fallout – the trauma and horror for women birthing "jellyfish babies", tiny transparent beings without bones and unable to survive this world, even 75 years since the bombs were detonated.[26] In Greenland, there is also a legacy of violence inflicted by colonial power and the military-industrial complex. Toward the end of the Cold War, the US left behind biological, chemical and radioactive waste after closing down the secret operations of Camp Century, an underground military base stretching for 3km (2 miles) under the ice. It was believed the waste would remain buried forever and no one would discover the toxic legacy left behind, except now the ice is melting faster than anyone predicted and the climate is heating faster in the Arctic than anywhere else on Earth. Each year is hotter than the one before in Greenland. In the winter of 2021, temperatures in the north of Greenland reached over 8°C (46°F), compared to the seasonal average of -20. A high of 13°C (55°F) was recorded in the capital, Nuuk, compared to the -5.3-degree average for that time of year. Simultaneously, temperatures rose to 40°C (104°F) above average in Antarctica. Before the end of the century, if the pace of melting continues, the toxic waste will be exposed.

Several years after watching Jetñil-Kijiner and Niviâna perform the poem "Rise", I asked Niviâna about her experience making the poem and her relationship with water and ice. She described her connection with water in such a cold and harsh climate as Greenland as an ambivalent connection, as water holds both a fascination and a terror for her.

"I find the sound of water very calming and at the same time looking into the deep ocean gives me a sense of anxiety," she said. "The unknown. It also fascinates me, because I feel connected to the planet when I think about how much water we consist of."

Niviâna grew up in the far north of Greenland in Upernavik in the 1990s, and much has changed since then. The Greenland ice sheet is the second largest mass of freshwater ice after Antarctica's ice sheet. New studies show the unprecedented rate of melting that has occurred in the last decade, raising global sea levels by over a quarter of an inch in that time. The ice sheet is no longer sustained by the accumulation of snowfall in the winter, and scientists believe that the rate of melting has already passed the point of no return.

Speaking of her earliest memory of water, Niviâna described walking on the crispy ice in -40°C (-40°F), recalling the vividness of the memory through her senses, and how her community's way of life was so interwoven with the story of the ice. "It has a certain sound and smell," she said. "I also combine the sound with the smell of gasoline, because in my hometown there were helicopters landing on ice and planes flying over the small town."

Glaciers are receding and disappearing completely all across the vast region. Niviâna's experience of travelling to the South of Greenland to witness how rapidly the glaciers are receding left a deep impact on her. Feeling the fragile state of the ice, literally shifting beneath her feet, with deep crevasses opening up and billions of tonnes of ice bleeding out in rivers of meltwater into the sea, heightened the sense of interdependence.

"We need to see nature as part of ourselves and not a foreign or other entity than ourselves," Niviâna told me. "We survive on this planet because of nature, but here we are destroying it. If you ask me, that is self-destructive behaviour. We talk about nature as this huge, certain mass of land, water, air or earth and I feel that we need to see it as a living, breathing thing. Because it is."

It is not just their islands that are experiencing the rapid and violent change of a warming climate, because if all the ice on Greenland were to melt, global sea levels would rise by 7m (23ft). In their poem, the two women asked if these cities would breathe underwater – Miami, New York, Amsterdam, Rio de Janeiro, Shanghai and Osaka – and understood the role of power. When I asked Niviâna what role women have to play in this warming future, she said *women* are well positioned because we understand the structure of power and how it is, when you are on the lower position of that power. "We know how to overcome a struggle from the bottom, going up," she said, "and I think that is crucial knowledge in terms of overcoming this climate crisis. And all the other crises we see in the world as well."

Jetñil-Kijiner also wrote about how the destruction and loss of land impacts the power of women. Marshall Islands society is matrilineal, where land and water rights are bestowed on women – power received by daughters from their mothers. What will happen, she asked, when there is no more land to pass down? When the water and soil is too toxic or the land drowned beneath the waves? What will happen to that power?

Niviâna left me with her understanding of ebb and flow, with ebb warning her of time running out. "I call it 'the urgency of everything'," she explained. "Now is the time for change and it also was yesterday." For her, flow means connection. "When you have the ice melting from our lands in Greenland, it is the same water that flows and washes away the shores of the Marshall Islands," she said. "We are all connected because we are one living, breathing thing; nature."

The final words the two women shouted out on the ice called on all of us to rise together:

"These issues affect each and every one of us
None of us is immune
And that each and every one of us has to decide
if we will rise."

EXERCISE:
MAPPING OUR CHANGING RELATIONSHIP WITH RISING WATERS

Group exercise 1: Story mapping

The Canadian Ocean Literacy Coalition, through a national online mapping platform called Stream2Sea, invites people to share stories of their connection with the ocean, how this connection may be changing due to rising sea levels and to consider how their values and emotions may be affected by these changes. These story maps also invite people to share what collective or personal actions may help to create what they ultimately want to see happen for the ocean. This is creating a national narrative of ocean connections and changing relationships.

You can create your own story map of your local catchment or coastal area by inviting members of your community to identify where they feel most connected to the water (a stream, river, lake or sea) and which changes they notice occurring. You could do this as a workshop with a large map of your catchment printed out with pins or sticky notes for participants to add their stories. Encourage people to bring along and share photos, videos, artwork, songs or dances that express their connection to the water. You could also use a digital mapping platform to create a virtual, ever-evolving story map of your community's changing relationship with water.

Here are some of the questions adapted from the Stream2Sea initiative that you could use as prompts:

- Where are you most connected to water?
- Which changes do you notice occurring there?
- What is your connection to water?
- Is your connection changing? If so, how?
- How may your values or emotions be affected by the change you identify?
- Who is most affected by the change in your story (non-human as well as human)?
- Why does the change in your story matter?
- What collective or personal actions and solutions could be taken that may help?
- What are the outcomes you ultimately want to see for the water?

Group exercise 2: River walk

A river walk is one way to consciously engage with the river, learn from it and better understand what is happening to the water at this time of climate crisis. During these walks it is also a time to reflect on our relationship with water and to share our knowledge about it in science, words, art or storytelling.

Take inspiration from the river guardians and organize your own river walk, following your local river from source to sea. This could be done during different seasons to improve your understanding of the course, catchment, ebb and flow of the river.

See the next chapter for how Basia Irland creates collective river walk experiences.

CHAPTER 7

HEART

Our heart is a vital organ and the first to develop in our body, helping to pump nutrients and oxygen to every single cell. There are over 40,000 neurons and neurotransmitters in the heart so it influences and interacts with our emotional state, which in turn influences its rhythm. The electromagnetic field of our heart can be felt at least a few feet outside of our body, communicating with the world around us.

In the same way that the heart's rhythm is altered by the music we listen to, it can also be altered by the ocean. Our heart rate slows when we come into contact with water, even simply splashing our faces with cold water in the morning – an evolutionary aquatic response that we share with marine mammals known as the mammalian dive response. Our heart may even synchronize with the sound of the sea, which is perhaps not so surprising since it contains over 70 per cent saltwater.

Water's healing powers

I first learned of the healing power of water from my grandmother, who was a devout Catholic. After every visit, as we crossed the threshold of her front door into the world outside, she would dip her finger into a full holy water font and would bless us, drawing the mark of the cross on our foreheads. Encouraging us to reciprocate, she lifted us up to dip our fingers into the font and bless her forehead in the same way. As I got older and whenever I was headed on a long journey, she would slip a bottle of holy water from one of her pilgrimages to Lough Derg, Lourdes or Medjugorje into my bag for my protection.

In later years, we would drive down to the local pier where she grew up and watch the changing weather move into the Donegal Bay, sweeping in from the open ocean on a strong westerly wind or softly rolling down from the mountains and dancing across the water. Watching the sea and breathing in the salty air was our favourite thing to do, a tonic for the soul. It was as if she intuitively knew how receptive water is and how it receives our prayers.

During my grandmother's last days, as she withdrew from this physical, material realm, the water in her body began to decrease too, no longer providing the building block for new cells or acting as a conduit for energy. It was as if, at the age of 92, her physical body had decided it was time to let go and release her soul. Before my eyes I was witnessing the gradual but steady breaking down of the body's capacity to repair itself. The self-healing mechanism had shut down and the only force that seemed to remain was prayer. Beside her bed was her bottle of holy water from Lourdes that she always kept near her.

It was impossible to move her anywhere, so I took her dry, leathery, feather-light hand in mine – it felt so delicate it was like holding a bird's wing – and told her we were going on a journey. "We are on the road to the sea, Granny," I said, describing the moment we were sharing in vivid images. "There is a gentle breeze and a still-warm autumn sun is shining. We can see the sea through the trees now and the sun is creating a glimmer path on the surface of the water that sparkles. Let's sit a while and watch the water.

It's moving gently today with a small swell rippling into the bay. Little waves make steady, gentle lapping sounds on the shore. The mountains beyond are a soft blue colour and the air smells fresh and salty. . ."

Her eyes were closed but as I spoke, my grandmother's face softened and she began to smile. Although this only lasted a few minutes, it felt, and still feels, like we spent her last afternoon on this Earth together picnicking by the sea watching the water, her favourite saying echoing in my ears: "The sea is a tonic for the soul." I was reminded of the words of the great Polynesian navigator, or wayfinder, Mau, who said, "If you can read the ocean, if you can see the island in your mind, you will never get lost." I felt my grandmother's ability to read the sea helped her find her way back to her heavenly home, free from earthly ties.

Sacred springs

Holy places such as Lourdes, where my grandmother made pilgrimages many times over the course of her life, are strongly associated with water. These religious places of worship often have ancient origins, with people drawn to the purity of the water in the healing wells for millennia. At Lourdes, the water is said to be full of vitality. Vital water has a healthy structure and is the most receptive, able to receive, store and transmit information or prayer. The holy wells of Lourdes are associated with the Mother Mary, and people go there to immerse themselves, seeking a cure for all kinds of illnesses and ailments.

Despite thousands of people entering the holy wells, a study of the structure and quality of the bathing waters discovered that all light frequencies were present, effectively neutralizing any pathogens.[1] One explanation is that the structure of the water in the wells is altered by the prayers of devotees and the loving energy offered up to Mother Mary. It would appear that the power of prayer purifies the water, and my grandmother always knew this.

Sacred wells and springs have long been associated with feminine power, and most were dedicated to a particular goddess. The oracle shrine of Delphi in Ancient Greece was built in 1400 BC around sacred springs believed to be the naval of the world. The names of the greatest of these springs, Lethe and Mnemosyne, "hint at water's power to help us forget our cares and remember what really matters," wrote Australian lecturer in gender and cultural studies, Astrida Neimanis.[2]

Ireland has the highest concentration of healing wells in Europe with over 3,000 documented across the landscape. These were once considered the vulvas of the Earth, a connection to the source of the goddess or entranceway into the womb of the Earth. Long before the scientific studies carried out at Lourdes, embedded within Indigenous cultures and many world religions is the belief that every time you acknowledge the spirit or life force of the water, be that through song, prayer or blessings, the healing powers of the water are activated and the water becomes medicine.

Ocean breath

Sofia, a physiotherapist in the UK with an interest in rehabilitation through surfing,, recently messaged me to share an unexpected experience of the power of our water connection to heal, especially when we consciously call upon it to help us. She told me how she brought the ocean into an Accident and Emergency room, where a person had decided to spend their end of life.

"I was called to see a patient to treat their chest, as they were struggling to breathe and to cough," Sofia wrote to me. "I knew this person was in palliation (reaching the end of their time). When I arrived at their bedroom where they were in bed surrounded by family, medical lines and attachments." After introducing herself, Sofia asked what she could do to help.

The patient replied, "I was hoping you could tell me." Then they spontaneously started to talk about their journey with cancer and about all the surgeries and medical procedures in great detail. What really helped, the patient said, was tai chi, but they could not remember the exercises.

Sofia asked the patient to close their eyes and focus on their breath, just feeling it as it was, without trying to change anything. She then proposed deepening the breath and engaging the senses – imagining a lovely smell going through the nostrils, which could be the smell of the ocean, if they liked the ocean.

"Oh, yeah, the ocean," the patient said smiling.

Sofia encouraged them to imagine a wave forming with the inbreath and then the wave rolling to the beach with the outbreath. She invited them to focus on the sounds of the waves, then introduced gentle movements such as those used in tai chi, circulating energy with the breath. When she had finished, she advised on different cough techniques and better positioning in their bed. She was thanked by the patient, who told her that the breathing exercises with tai chi and thinking about the ocean really helped.

Sofia shared with me that she was inspired by the power of visualization as a way to connect with the ocean wherever we are. She was surprised and excited by how the simple practice optimized comfort for the patient she was treating. "It was amazing that the ocean wellbeing effects can be brought to an A&E department," she wrote.

I was deeply moved by how this mirrored my own experience with my grandmother, and how our connection to the ocean could help us on our ultimate journey and crossing over when death is near.

Shortly after that experience, Sofia returned to the ocean to reconnect with the embodied feeling of joy she knew it gave her but had long neglected in her own life. She even took up surfing and discovered a different way of listening to her body and the sea. Inspired by these experiences, she met with her seniors in the NHS to discuss potential for a "blue health" project with the community neurorehabilitation team for people with neurological conditions. She wrote again to tell me that even if she keeps having "wipeouts", she won't resist the force of the wave or the challenge, and will let herself soften and come afloat to begin again with new lessons learned.

The power of visualization

In the report "Aboriginal Women, Water and Health", Indigenous grandmother Ellen White shared how water will agree to help us with anything we ask of it, if we acknowledge it. One way to do that is to awaken our connection with water through the power of visualization. When activating our connection with the ocean through our breath and our senses, for example, our brain believes that we really are immersed by the sea, and our body begins to respond physically as if we are there.

Scientific studies have shown the positive effects of creative visualization on health, such as improving immunity, reducing stress, healing and pain management, such as in Sofia's story. Science also shows that visualization improves many facets of life, from athletic ability to cognitive performance, to attention, to states of flow, to self-esteem. As I mentioned in Chapter 3, when competing in surfing I used vivid, highly detailed internal images, or neuroimaging, that took me through the entire performance from the start of my competition to the end. I engaged all my senses and combined my knowledge of the sports venue and the particular type of waves that broke there into this mental rehearsal. This would prime my body and mind for the actual performance.

Visualization is powerful because it is considered to be a high-leverage practice, meaning that by consistently committing short amounts of time, even five minutes a day, it can have a profound effect. Brain studies now reveal that thoughts produce the same mental instructions as actions. Visualization helps our brain to send a signal to our body to start behaving in a way consistent with the images in our mind. It creates a very real body–mind connection so that we actually begin to experience the benefits of being by our favourite water or immersed in the water, from wherever we are. As described in Chapter 3, this became a critical tool during the successive lockdowns of the Covid-19 pandemic and remains a vital practice during such uncertain times and in our increasingly urbanized lives.

By creating new nerve pathways, or rewiring our neural network, visualization can help us get out of mind-ruts we may find ourselves stuck in. As an exercise, it can be a wonderful reset tool, helping to build our resilience muscles, the ability to bounce back after a disruption or to respond to change, and is instantly accessible, requiring absolutely nothing other than your imagination. I share a guided visualization at the end of this chapter to help you get started.

Restoring our ocean heart

Throughout this book, the complex story of water as a place of paradox has been highlighted; the power of water to destroy life as well as create life, blue spaces as places of danger as well as healing, and the growing threats caused by our changing relationship with water in terms of pollution, extraction, climate change, (un)natural disasters, forced migration, water security and scarcity. For the first time, in its 2022 report, the Intergovernmental Panel on Climate Change (IPCC) acknowledged colonization as the root cause of climate instability, with growing inequities heightening climate risks.[3]

Colonization is also at the root of our deteriorating relationship with water, although this is often not clearly or explicitly addressed in conversations, research and discourse related to the benefits of "blue spaces", of the restorative power of water for human health and wellbeing. As discussed in my introduction, inequalities in how we might access or engage with blue spaces limit the ability to experience "blue mind" or any of the other myriad psychological, physical, emotional and spiritual benefits explored in this book.

For many, especially those who have been marginalized, various water environments may come to represent places of trauma and traumatic events that can make it very difficult to learn to love these places. A powerful example of this is in the communities that survived the devastating Indian Ocean tsunami of 2004, killing 250,000 people in a dozen countries, and where four times as many women as men lost their lives. This was due to a complex mix of factors, including strict sociocultural rules and norms that control the lives, agency and mobility of women in particular, limiting their capacities to escape to safety.

Women lack access to swimming and water safety skills in Asia, as in many other regions of the world, and their care-taking responsibilities affect their ability to flee, as well as having a lack of access to resources that aid escape such as transport or money. In addition, post-disaster levels of violence against women also increase. The failure to understand the gender and context-specific needs and vulnerabilities of women, especially in climate- or disaster-related scenarios, risks the lives of many.

Many coastal communities experienced heightened post-traumatic stress symptoms, especially for the most vulnerable – children, young women and widows. How can we transform such a traumatizing environment, the ocean, where the dominant perception is one of risk and danger, into a safe and healing space? How can our relationship with the ocean be transformed from a fearful one into a loving one?

This is what some of the pioneering female surfers in Sri Lanka set out to accomplish when they established SeaSisters, a remarkable story of how psychological transformation can occur even in places of trauma. SeaSisters is a women's social enterprise that creates a safe space for Sri Lankan girls and women to foster a love for the ocean through their swim and surf programmes, as well as equipping them with the skills needed to work in the surf tourism industry. Cofounder Martina Burtscher told me the story of Mona, who she interviewed as part of her master's degree thesis in 2017 when local Sri Lankan women first began to take up surfing, to understand what role surfing might play in the empowerment of Sri Lankan women in a society where surfing was highly masculinized and the domain of men.

Mona lost her mother in the tsunami and this left her so deeply traumatized that she had avoided going near the sea for years. For her, it was a place of tragedy, fear and loss. After much encouragement from friends, she eventually agreed to join her first surf lesson at a programme called "Girls Make Waves". Despite feeling extremely nervous, with the support of the other women and girls in the group, she managed to ride her first waves lying on her belly. She later described her experience, saying, "There was some kind of energy coming into my heart."[4]

This energy continued to grow and Mona kept surfing, wanting to catch her own wave. Eventually surfing made her forget about the terror of the tsunami and became a way to manage stress in her life; the ocean had become a source of fun, pleasure and social connection with other women who all shared a bond. The more time Mona spent in the sea and surf, the more she wanted to learn about the ocean and today she still surfs and is even teaching her two daughters.

There are many more stories and testimonials from Sri Lankan female surfers who participate in SeaSisters ocean-based programmes that speak about this transformative power of the ocean. Kalpa, a translator and member of SeaSisters, shared how she began to realize she missed the ocean, even though she lived near it her whole life. Swimming and surfing had given her that deeper, more intimate connection. She even started to go for beach walks with her mother, something she had never done before. Sanu, a rising star in Sri Lankan surfing, said in a 2021 documentary film about her (called *We Are Like Waves*) that she "found herself in the ocean".[5]

Our blue hearts

There is a growing body of research revealing the effects of water on the brain, such as an increase in alpha waves when people are more immersed in water environments – these brain waves described in Chapter 1 are associated with a more restful state and greater openness or the ability to absorb new information and think more creatively. There has been significantly less research on the relationship between our engagement with blue spaces and our hearts.

Some studies have primarily focused on elite endurance athletes testing the limits of cold water immersion on human physiology, including the heart. In these controlled study settings, cold water immersion and swimming were associated with health indicators such as better sleep quality and improved vascular functioning – the circulation of the blood around the body. Indeed, much has been examined when it comes to the impact of the mammalian dive response on the human body in free divers, in particular bradycardia, the slowing of the heart rate when we are immersed in water. At the same time, immersion in cold water can constrict blood vessels, pushing blood flow toward the heart, increasing blood pressure. For an unhealthy heart, cold exposure can pose a serious risk, which is why it is important to slowly become acclimatized to the temperature of the water. Over time, this shift in blood flow actually regulates blood pressure.

The world's best and most natural free divers, the *ama* or "women of the sea" of Japan and Korea, who spend their whole lives free diving to hunt for shellfish on a single breath, have remarkable vascular function, akin to that of other marine mammals. It would seem their hearts have adapted to all the time spent diving under water, a tradition passed on from mother to daughter for millennia.

I wonder if the relative lack of research on the interrelationship between water and the heart, an organ that is over 70 per cent water, is symbolic of modern society's tendency to be led by the head rather than the heart. There is an obsession with the brain and cognitive "performance" and how we can become more "productive", suppressing our emotions to think our way out of problems, rather than feeling into what is most alive in us and being led by our heart. There is also much evidence on how the sound of ocean or water regulates our nervous system, altering our brain waves and releasing a flood of neurochemicals that increase blood flow to our heart as well as our brain, causing our whole body to relax.

Wonders of the ocean's hearts

On this planet, the biggest heart in the ocean belongs to the blue whale, which can reach up to 30.5m (100ft) in length – the largest animal ever to have lived. The blue whale's heartbeat is so strong that it can be detected 3km (2 miles) away, although the human ear is not sensitive enough to pick it up unaided. Infrasound waves, which permeate the ocean world, resonate at a frequency undetectable to human ears but are still believed to trigger emotional and somatic sensations in our body.

I wonder if there was a time when the blue whale was so plentiful that the ocean resonated with the rhythm of their heartbeat. The ocean would have also been full of their "whale song". With the loss of so many whale populations to whaling and a mixture of threats driven by the unwanted intimacy with our material, consumer culture, we have created what author and journalist Rebecca Giggs calls "an aquatic 'Silent Spring'".[6] Giggs has written about the unique "biophony" each whale group and population creates – a term for environmental soundscapes. We are replacing this biophony with an artificial cacophony of noise that is drowning out every cubic metre of ocean. Researchers are beginning to associate the complex ways in which whales communicate by sound as a form of "whale culture". Each group of cetaceans teaches each other new songs and hunting strategies like traditions passed down from generation to generation, and there is evidence that they create new customs in response to changes in their environment. If we could see our planet through the lens of the culture of other species, could it change our relationships with other species and nature?

Sperm whales, once portrayed as monstrous giants of the sea and hunted relentlessly for their oil, are shy, gentle and highly social creatures with the largest brain of any animal on this planet. They live in matrilineal societies led by the older matriarchs. Science is revealing that sperm whales have dialects that are unique to groups of families and don't intermingle with sperm whales that have a different language. Their language sounds like a complex series of Morse code-like clicks, or "codas", that biologists believe the animals learn from their mothers. Sperm whale clans will also assign a "babysitter", usually a younger female, when they are deepdiving for food, much in the same way humans would.

Orca, arguably the most intelligent beings in the ocean, create unique feeding strategies depending on where in the world they live. Elders are of great importance in a family group, with orca young living five times longer in clans with grandmothers. Orca mothers, and other whales, have been documented carrying their calves and/or stillborns, unable to let them go for days – it is hard to interpret this in any other way than a profound expression of grief. Orca, wrote Giggs, do not just have a culture but have cultural diversity. Distinct groups (called ecotypes) have been identified with their own unique social behaviours, food preferences and ways of communicating or making sound. This changes the way we think about single species conservation and highlights the importance of protecting the greatest range and diversity of contexts that allow this kind of diversity to flourish.

At the UN World Oceans Day conference in 2021, wildlife photographer Brian Skerry described how the use of passive cameras are able to create a window into social behaviours of beluga.[7] Beluga whales have a "group maternity ward", a particular place where the mothers will go to birth their young at a particular site. Newborn beluga are given the same name as the mother until they are able to fend for themselves and then they get their own name. They also love to play, picking up a flat rock and carrying it before dropping it for another beluga to pick it up. Despite all the challenges they face, they still make time for play.

Interspecies collaboration has also been observed, especially between bottlenose dolphins and humans. In Ancient Greece, these relationships were captured in myths and even depicted on coins. Since 1847, a group of bottlenose dolphins off the coast of Brazil has been voluntarily cooperating with human fishermen to help them capture fish by "herding" the shoals into their nets. That said, Giggs warned that we are capable of loving an animal to death too. Unregulated, overcrowded tourist experiences that sell encounters with wild cetaceans disturb their feeding and mating habits. Part of a whale's charisma is their mystery – that they are these rarely seen, majestic leviathans of a deep otherworld – except now they are coming into almost constant unwanted contact with the consequences of our consumer culture, many carrying the traces of it in their bellies.

Water ceremony

At the beginning of 2020, before any of us knew how the future would unfold, I found myself in unfamiliar territory. I was headed to the Treaty Truckhouse on the Shubenacadie River that belonged to the water protectors. Mi'kmaq elder, water walker, water protector and residential school survivor Dorene Bernard had invited me to a peace pipe and water ceremony to offer our support and solidarity to water protectors at sacred places threatened by Big Oil and multinational and political interests not only in Nova Scotia but across Canada, North America and in Indigenous communities all around the world.

Dorene is one of the leaders of the self-proclaimed "Grassroots Grandmothers", and an essential force in the campaign to "Stop Alton Gas", a natural gas company that wanted to create salt caverns to store liquefied natural gas (LNG) and dump the brine waste in the Shubenacadie River. The Alton Gas website states: "During construction of the caverns, brine will be released into a constructed channel connected to the Shubenacadie River where it will mix with the tidal (brackish) river water to maximize dilution."

The amount of salt from these caverns amounts to over eight million cubic yards – 500,000 dump truck loads – depending on how many caverns are created. There are concerns that not only will this destroy one of the last breeding grounds for striped bass and the habitat for endangered Atlantic salmon who use these waterways, but that it might also open the way for further fracking. In addition to the social, economic and environmental threat, the Alton Gas project is another example of ongoing colonization of Indigenous people and natural resources, where huge, industrial-scale "energy projects" are being pushed through Indigenous communities without free, prior and informed consent.

Treaty Truckhouse was built thanks to Dorene's resourcefulness and wisdom of the history and rights of her people – the Sipekne'katik First Nation, and their ancestral connection to the water and the land. It is an important demonstration of resistance to both the government's failure to consult with Sipekne'katik First Nation and Alton Gas, who legally must honour the Mi'kmaq treaty right to fish.

That night, however, we were gathering for a different form of protest, one that deeply embodied the sacred feminine, the moon and the water, to pray for the water and the healing and protection of all water protectors. "As women," Dorene said to me, "we are the natural water keepers; it is from our waters that we bring forth life and the ability to create."

I had only just met Dorene a few days before at the regional North Atlantic workshop for the United Nations Decade of Ocean Science for Sustainable Development in the capital city of Nova Scotia, Halifax. I could still feel the words of her opening address ringing inside me like a bell, encouraging all the VIP policy and science delegates to connect with the spirit of water within us and all around us. She spoke of water's aliveness and sacredness, its power to sense and feel us, and the pivotal role that women must play as waterkeepers in all decision-making when it comes to protecting water.

A mixture of Grassroots Grandmothers and their supporters, many of them young students from Halifax, had gathered to help prepare food and offerings. Like many who survived the residential schools, Dorene had only begun her journey to reclaim her heritage and the wisdom of her people much later in life, after becoming a mother. She explained that she was still learning and why the embodiment of these practices and having ceremony was so important – as a way to reclaim lost wisdom and to actively engage with and honour the power of water, water as life, and water as spirit.

A sacred bundle was created to offer to the river, to protect all the water protectors who gave so much to the water and all the life it nourishes. We stood outside in the knee-deep snow, the moon glowing above and the slushy, near-frozen river slowly moving below us. We sang a water prayer, and Dorene's daughter cast the offering into the river.

Singing or prayer is one way to cultivate a deeper connection and, as Lakota skier Connor Ryan explained to me, to introduce ourselves to the water as another conscious being, as a relative, and to show respect to the water. Communicating in this way allows water to sense us, what we are saying and feeling, as much as we sense it. This is a really valuable attitude to cultivate that helps us realize that every action we take has an impact on water and the places that hold the water.

Water songs

The water song has a long history and there are many women's water songs from different cultures and nations. Not long after that visit to Nova Scotia, I came across the Algonquin Water Song. It was born from the 2002 Circle of All Nations Gathering, at Kitigan Zibi Anishinabeg in Ottawa, Canada, where the Grandmothers and Elders decided to write a song that women attending the gathering would learn and spread throughout the world. They created a website as a resource and shared a beautifully recorded video of generations of women singing the water song, in light of the grave dangers our waters are facing everywhere and to hasten the teaching and widen the circle. The lyrics are sung four times, each facing one of the four directions in this order: east, south, west and north. These are the phonetic lyrics:

Nee bee wah bow
En die en
Aah key mis kquee
Nee bee wah bow
Hey ya hey ya hey ya hey
Hey ya hey ya hey ya ho[8]

The song is sung like a lullaby because of the important role of water at birth. Algonquin Grandmother Nancy Andry is quoted on the website saying, "The song means the water is the life's blood of our mother, the Earth. Water is the life's blood of our own bodies."[9]

Water plays a deeply feminine role throughout our life cycle, especially for women. It is used in rituals across cultures to welcome newborns and in naming ceremonies, marriages and death rites. It also has an important role at coming-of-age or puberty ceremonies for young women. I came across a powerful passage in the report on Aboriginal Women, Water and Health, in which Ellen describes her own puberty passage.[10] She was taken to the ocean and met the rushing waters between the rocks and became lodged in one place and then "unstuck" with the assistance of the water. The experience provided her with healing gifts that she would carry and draw upon throughout her lifetime.

Menarche, a girl's first bleed, is often not celebrated in modern, western culture, although it is beginning to make a comeback. Around the time of my menarche, I was competing nationally as an athlete in surfing and swimming. I had a lot of support from my mother but it still felt like menstruation was something to keep concealed as a young girl in sports. There was no support, education or information about how to manage my periods when competing, doing watersports, travelling and training. It was best not spoken of, let alone celebrated, but I realize now that an awareness of natural biorhythms has always influenced every aspect of my life. As a woman who surfs, I naturally move with the tides, and since early childhood I was already attuned to the rhythms of my local environment.

I understand that the cycles of the planetary bodies affect individual bodies and moods. I was born on a new moon, and an awareness of the lunar cycle and its influence on me and my environment was instilled in me from an early age. My cycle is also inextricably linked to the sea and the ebb and flow of tides. This awareness was very much embedded in my way of life since childhood and as a lifelong surfer. I have only begun to consciously link and map the influence of sea, tides, sun and moon to my menstrual cycle in more recent years, and charting my cycle has now become part of my daily routine and a practice that I find very grounding.

Understanding water values

In our everyday lives, how do we recognize that all water is connected and all life is connected to water? That the water in my teacup, in my body, in the sky, in the rivers and the ocean, are all one. Do we realize we are held in a "liquid embrace",[11] to quote writer and ecofeminist Starhawk; that what happens to any one part of the water affects all of us? In the words of feminist scholar Astrida Neimanis, we need to "enact an ethics of curiosity and care".[12] We need to understand that water belongs to no one but itself – an ethics of care that is open and willing to learn from other aquatic organisms, rather than reducing them to economic stockpiles of resources and "materials in service of the human project".

How instead might we become aquatic-minded? Holly Jean Buck, New York professor of the environment and sustainability, believes in a radical overhaul of how we teach our children. "Imagine," she wrote, "a primary education where students spend time learning to relate and think with other species; learning from traditional ecological knowledge as well as other forms of science."[13] A deepening of our understanding of and engagement with other forms of being, especially from the sea out of which we first emerged, "could help expand our embodied capacities, reconfigure who and what constitutes 'us'". Buck argues that these multispecies experiences would foster ecological care, helping us in "becoming experts in connection with a whole".

In addition to her Receding/Reseeding project, another example of connecting to the whole is the Gathering of Waters project, the brainchild of eco-artist Basia Irland in collaboration with communities of scientists, artists, activists, students, outdoor guides and farmers along waterways all over the world. For decades, Irland has travelled along the length of rivers from source to sea, including the 1,875-mile Rio Grande with its source in the mountains of Colorado to where it merges with the sea in the Gulf of Mexico in Boca Chica.

The journey took five years and involved a series of practices that actively engaged hundreds of participants in creating a narrative, or repository, for the river. This included each participant pouring a small amount of river water into a river vessel canteen and writing in a logbook before physically passing these along to the next person downstream. In this way, everyone involved created a human river that brought an awareness of downstream effects. When the canteen reached the end of the river, participants released the waters during a ceremony offering gratitude and respect. At the end, the collection of the river vessels, logbooks, water analysis, maps, photos and videos formed "Repositories".

This project has activated what Irland refers to as a watershed consciousness, where there is a deeper awareness of the interconnectedness between all who live along the river. The Gathering of Waters is a way to help build back relations with the river, and between communities dependent on the river, by creating a shared bond with the water.

Respecting water's value

With most waterways in the world struggling, water is also in need of healing. A woman who recognizes this and has committed her work to creating water remedy interventions is Irish artist and water healer Ruth le Gear. Le Gear has spent time quite literally immersed in various bodies of water and with water in all its forms: liquid, vapour and ice. She wrote in an essay on her website that her first conversation with any place she encounters is with the water there. Water holds the memories of all that passes through it, the history, knowledge and energy of place throughout time.

Through an embodied practice, she examines the qualities of the water and the memories held within it. Her remedy-making process uses methods of serial dilution, such as in homoeopathy, to release the water's memories and potential. As well as making healing remedies that are offered back to the water, Le Gear makes remedies with healing potential from the water, such as a remedy made from a calving glacier's water in the Arctic. Le Gear describes this as an essence for transformation – coming from the moment an iceberg was formed, "releasing the past and bearing witness to the last phase of life".

Even though we may not all be able to access or go to these wilder or free-flowing water bodies, we may be able to work with water in our everyday, modern settings. For some, the first step may be simply acknowledging the water in your shower and its power to cleanse and heal.

It is also possible to learn to work with the energies from the water that comes out of your tap, always beginning with giving it your intentions of gratitude and respect. The Indigenous grandmothers interviewed for the report on Aboriginal Women, Water and Health stressed that water carries spirit energy wherever it is, be that in mountains, the human body or out of the shower. The reciprocal relationship between people and water is largely absent in a modern society that has bottled, packaged and commodified water. The way to begin to restore that relationship is to give thanks and appreciate the water for what it offers.

With a shared reliance on the global ocean, this could be our great unifier if it were free from our human borders. Visual storyteller from the Secwepemc and Syilx Nations of British Columbia, Dorothy Christian, and poet and waterkeeper Rita Wong wrote in *Downstream: Reimagining Water* that contemplating our relationship with the ocean "offers us a way to scale up to the larger collective questions of humanity's future, which is intimately dependent on how we navigate our relationship with water in generations to come".[14]

Water, its aliveness, how it circulates, moves and breathes, is the pattern that connects us to all life. In a way, this book has also encouraged different ways of noticing patterns and reading water, ways of sensing and being like water that also allow us to move with greater flow. When I was competing as a professional surfer, I took time before the competition began to observe the patterns of waves breaking at a particular surf spot. I would draw in the sand how the waves behaved: where they broke, how often, how many, which one was the most powerful in a set or "train" of waves, the time between the pulse of each wave. This exercise would be repeated at different stages of the tide, or if the wind changed direction, which would invariably alter the shape, pattern and behaviour of the waves. Eventually, I would have a feel for the pattern of waves that broke on any given day, a pattern I could become part of and participate in.

In practice, this kind of embodied observation, noticing and listening can support moments of flow in the surf, when mind–body–wave all seem to be in sync. It also helps to create a richer connection to the environment, or a sense of *dhúchas*. There is no Irish word for landscape, which would suggest a separateness, and *dhúchas* is the closest meaning. Often translated as heritage, it represents a sense of place and belonging that is much more alive and dynamic to Irish speakers, a natural affinity. *Filleadh ar do dhúchas* means "to return home, to where one belongs, to revert to kind" – a return to the waters that birthed us.[15] This reconnection with water creates intimacy, dispelling the distance.

Welcoming water into our hearts

I have experienced so often how water can completely dispel the distance between people, freeing us from our social awkwardness of fear of judgement. One such experience was on a mizzly morning in early February, where the rain falls in continuous misty sheets where the clouds have dropped to the Earth. The Irish word for this type of rain is *salachar ceo*. A small group had come together from different parts of Ireland to celebrate Imbolc, or "i mbolg" in Old Irish, meaning "in the belly". Imbolc is an ancient Irish festival with Celtic origins that honours the return of the light and slow emergence of new life and growth after a long dark winter.

We gathered next to the bank of the Glenaniff River and stood huddled and damp while the local custodian shared his insights on the river's history and explained how to read it. I guided everyone in a short meditation as a way to begin the journey from our heads into our bodies and to begin to sense and connect with the river.

There was a strong flow of water running after the heavy rains from the night before and I could feel the anticipation and nervousness of the group. The roar and hum of the multiple waterfalls and rapids kept everyone quiet, for fear their voices would be snatched away. As we followed our river guide, scouting our way upstream, it seemed it might be impossible to get into the river for a swim in one of the rock pools. The flow looked too strong and most people had never immersed themselves in a river before.

Just as we were about to give up on the idea, a smaller waterfall on the edge of the riverbank spilling over a sheer 8ft (2.5m) wall of dark, moss-covered limestone rock and onto a mossy ledge drew the attention of one of the group members. This looked like the most natural place in the world to take a shower. We had missed it on the way up, being drawn by the more dramatic, turbulent features of the river. Next to this "daughter" waterfall was the much larger "mother" waterfall that had formed a deep womb-like plunge pool of water below the rock ledge. The clockwise swirl of the water meant it was possible to gently slide our bodies from the mossy ledge into the water and be carried around the pool in a wide circle before being deposited back where we started, held in a watery embrace.

The more we closed the distance between us and the water, stripping off our warm clothes, standing barefoot on the wet, squelchy leaf litter and picking our way gingerly over the saturated, spongy moss toward the falling water, the more the subdued energy of the group shifted. It was as if contact with the vitality of the water opened up something in our bodies that freed our energy, our own vitality pouring out in response, uncensored and unashamed, in shrieks, howls, roars and laughter. There was a reverence to each person's approach to the water and initial contact with the shock of cold, the different ways we sought to connect with it or feel it on our skin, entering the waterfall as if receiving a blessing or a kiss. The giggling joy of being gently swirled in the pool, as if we, too, had become bubbling, bouncing water molecules. The incredible feeling of intimacy of the fresh, earthy, cold water on bare skin dispelled the distance between one another, the water bonding us. For the rest of the day together, we remained open and connected, carrying the memory of the water with us long after we left.

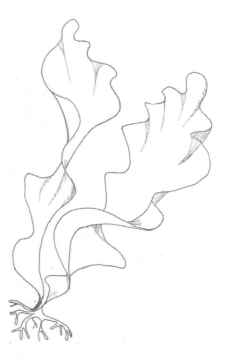

EXERCISE:
RECONNECTING WITH OUR HEART

Blue heart visualization

Self-care is not a replacement for social care. It does not mean not pushing ourselves out of comfort zones but instead it means coming into closer encounter with ourselves: the aliveness, richness and fullness of all that we are and of the living world around us. There is often a greater emphasis on the brain/mind when it comes to our mental health and in practices such as meditation and visualization.

This visualization helps to reconnect you with your heart and explore how your heart influences your brain, body and emotional state.

- Get comfortable and lie down so you can completely surrender – closing your eyes will help you access a deeper state of relaxation and to drop into your imagination. Remember, if your mind wanders at any stage during the visualization, that is totally okay. Whenever you notice this, just bring your attention back to your breath. That in itself is an act of mindfulness.
- Take a moment to arrive (ground yourself). Then begin by noticing and settling into your body, and think about the sensations in your body.
- Follow your breath. . . in. . . and out. . . and allow it to soften your body, letting your body sink into the floor

to be held. Notice the ebb and flow of your breath. . .
moving your body – rising and falling. . .

- From this place, bring your awareness to your heart. You
  may want to place a hand over your heart, noticing where
  it is and how it is cushioned between your lungs, a little
  bigger than the size of your fist.
- Sense your heart's beat – its rhythmic pulse.
- Place a hand on your belly and notice your breath.
- Feel the sense of expansion in your body as you breathe
  in. . . and the feeling of release and letting go on the
  exhale. The expansion and contraction of your lungs as
  you breathe gently massages your heart.
- Feel the gentle rise and fall of your belly as you breathe,
  mirroring the ebb and flow of the tides.
- Imagine your body floating, effortlessly held and
  supported by warm water, relaxing and softening with
  each breath.
- Now imagine your heart holding a swirling palette of
  watercolours inside it. These colours are waiting to
  be released by your breath, pumped from your heart
  outward in different directions, travelling to every part of
  your body, painting it in deep colourful hues.
- Allow your breath to flow freely now, into your
  entire body.
- As you inhale, letting your belly rise, your oxygen-rich
  breath soaks up the colours from your heart, the colours
  spreading across your chest and up to the crown of
  your head.
- On your next breath, the muscles of your heart reach for
  another colour. Feel the warm pigment flow across your

forehead, eyelids, cheeks, nose, around the curve of your jaw and down your neck.

- Allow the breath to reach for more colour, gently released and pumped from the heart. The palette of watercolours are spreading across your shoulders, down your arms, flowing through your wrists and across the palms of your hands, trickling into each and every fingertip.
- As you breathe into your rainbow-filled heart, let the colours release and expand around your torso, travelling down your spine: violet, indigo, blue, all swirling around each vertebra.
- Dip into your palette again and notice the paint moving through your navel, the wash of colours flowing into your pelvis and spilling over your hip bones.
- Feel the sensation of the various colours flowing down your thighs, around your knees and down to your ankles. Then swirling around the numerous, tiny bones of your feet and trickling into your toes.
- Now sense the colours spreading further outward with each pulse of your heart beyond your body and into the water around you.
- Notice the detail of this watercolour your heart is painting as it expands out from your body: heart, toes, fingertips, crown of your head, all flowing and swirling out into the water.
- Take a moment to be with this image as you breathe gently into your belly, soaking up the beauty of what your heart has created.
- Give thanks for all that your heart does for you.

- Allow yourself to fully receive all that you have created and experienced.
- Slowly begin to bring your awareness back to your breath, feeling the gentle rise and fall of your body.
- Take a deep breath in, and let it go.
- Begin to bring movement back into your body, wriggling your fingers and toes, maybe stretching your body out. . . and gently blinking your eyes open.
- If you were lying down, slowly come back to a seated position.
- On your next breath, take a slow deep inhalation and release it, with a big sigh. Notice how you feel.

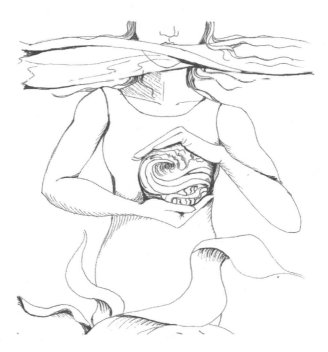

CULTIVATING INNER EBB AND FLOW

Our relationship with water is broken. In today's modern society, much of our water bodies, rivers and seas have become degraded, polluted and silenced and we have forgotten how to listen to them. The story of power and dominion over water does not serve us or the planet well. This book has shared new ways of relating to water, and new stories of reconnection. It has revealed the importance of an "ethics of encounter",[1] a way of being with water that goes beyond a controlling and extractive interaction, instead embracing the value of bringing play, love and intention into that relationship.

I hope this book has given you some insights and wisdom that will help you live a more connected life. The creative ecological practices I have shared ask us what we can learn from water and bring attention to the diversity of ways that we are mutually shaped and formed with and through our waterways and waterscapes. Water acts as a powerful mirror – in it, we see ourselves and are reminded of our capacity to be like water; of our remarkable potential to recover and return to wholeness, to move fluidly and find flow, and our ability to embrace the unknown. Water teaches us the power of presence, the value of feeling and being with all of who we are so that we may act with greater clarity and empathy.

The water protectors and guardians in this book remind us that we belong to the water, we don't own it, and we are obliged to care for it. I hope you feel inspired to form a relationship with your local living water systems. Make a commitment to your water to get to know it and listen to it, to cherish and protect it, and in turn to become known by the water and all that it gives life to. Our health and the health of this blue Earth depends on it.

NOTES

Any quote that doesn't have an endnote was told to me directly in person, over a phone or video interview.

Introduction

1 "Blue Health", bluehealth2020.eu/
2 Strang, Veronica, quoted in: Ronan Foley, et al (eds). *Blue Space, Health and Wellbeing*, Routledge, 2019, p23
3 Nichols, Wallace J, *Blue Mind*, Little, Brown and Company, 2014
4 Ryrie, Charlie, *The Healing Energies of Water*, Gaia, 1998, p13
5 Bayo Akomolafe speaking at the Concrete Love Festival, Lisbon, 30 November 2021
6 Ryrie, Charlie, p14
7 "Are We Running Out of Water?", theworldcounts.com
8 Leonard, Kelsey, "Why lakes and rivers should have the same rights as humans", *TED Talk*, 2019, www.ted.com/speakers/kelsey_leonard
9 Ryrie, Charlie, p58
10 Schwenk, Theodor, *Sensitive Chaos*, Rudolf Steiner Press (2nd Ed), 2014
11 Benveniste, Jacques, et al, "Human basophil degranulation triggered by very dilute antiserum against IgE". *Nature*, 333, 1988, p816–18
12 Sanderson, Darlene, quoted in "A report from the Indigenous World Forum on Water and Peace", *Indigenous Message on Water*, 2014, p19 and p94
13 Gundle, Leo and Atkinson, Amelia, "Pregnancy, cold water swimming and cortisol: The effect of cold water swimming on obstetric outcomes", *Medical Hypotheses*, 144, 2020

Chapter 1. Connection

1 Francis, Gavin, *Island Dreams*, Canongate Books, 2020
2 Dabiri, Emma, *What White People Can Do Next*, Penguin Books, 2021
3 Heke, Ihirangi, *Atua Matua Māori Health Framework*, 2014, toitangata.co.nz/wp-content/uploads/2017/06/Dr_Ihi_Heke_Atua_Matua_Framework.pdf
4 Kasket, Elaine, *All the Ghosts in the Machine*, Hachette, 2019
5 Tsui, Bonnie, *Why We Swim*, Algonquin Books, 2020, p221
6 Cox, Lynne, quoted in Tsui, Bonnie p222
7 Reinhart, RJ, "Majority Worldwide Cannot Swim; Most of Them Are Women", *Gallup*, 2021, news.gallup.com/opinion/gallup/352679/majority-worldwide-cannot-swim-women.aspx
8 Porges, Stephen, *The Polyvagal Theory*, W. W. Norton & Company, 2011
9 Surfers Against Sewage, *Thriving Ocean, Thriving People: The Connection Between Ocean Restoration and the Blue Wellbeing Economy*, 2020, www.sas.org.uk/wp-content/uploads/SAS-OceanRecoveryReport2021-Digital.pdf
10 Tsui, Bonnie, p67
11 Calidas, Tamsin, "Reading *I Am an Island*: Film and Reading", Instagram post, 7 August 2021
12 Mandamin, Josephine, quoted in Anderson, Kim, "Aboriginal Women, Water and Health: Reflections from Eleven First Nations, Inuit, and Métis Grandmothers", *Atlantic Centre of Excellence for Women's Health and Prairie Women's Health Centre of Excellence*, 2010, p12
13 Ulrich, Roger, "Natural versus urban scenes: Some psychophysiological effects", *Environment and Behavior*, 13(5), 1981, pp523–556
14 Gascon, M. et al, "Outdoor blue spaces, human health and well-being: A systematic review of quantitative studies", *Hygiene and Environmental Health*, 220(8), 2017, pp1207–1221
15 Buxton, R. T. et al, "A synthesis of health benefits of natural sounds and their distribution in national parks", *Proceedings of the National Academy of Sciences*, 118(14), 2021
16 Tsui, Bonnie, p73
17 White, M P, et al, "Blue space, health and well-being: A narrative overview and synthesis of potential benefits", *Environmental Research*, 191, 2020

18 Throsby, Karen, "'If I go in like a cranky sea lion, I come out like a smiling dolphin': marathon swimming and the unexpected pleasures of being a body in water", *Feminist Review*, 103(1), 2013, p5

19 Carlin, Caitríona et al, "Research Report 348: Nature and Environment to Attain and Restore Health (NEAR Health)", *Environmental Protection Agency*, 2020, www.epa.ie/publications/research/environment--health/ Research_Report_348.pdf

20 Tanaka, H, "Swimming Exercise", *Sports Medicine*, 39(5), 2009, pp377–387

21 "The Sensing Nature Project", sensing-nature.com

22 Gilmore, Heath, "'Simply mind-blowing': blind surfer Matt Formston's wave of glory", *Sydney Morning Herald*, 26 July 2021, www.smh.com.au/national/nsw/simply-mind-blowing-blind-surfer-matt-formston-s-wave-of-glory-20210531-p57wvn.html

23 Polacca, Mona, quoted in Christian, D. and Wong, R. (eds) *Downstream*, Wilfrid Laurier University Press, 2017, p78

24 Shubin, Neil, *Your Inner Fish*, Vintage, 2009

25 Batmanghelidj, Fereydoon, *Your Body's Many Cries for Water*, Tagman Press, 2000

26 "Aboriginal Women, Water and Health", 2010, p8

27 Fainu, Kalolaine, "'Shark calling': locals claim ancient custom threatened by seabed mining", *The Guardian*, 30 September 2021, www.theguardian.com/world/ 2021/sep/30/sharks-hiding-locals-claim-deep-sea-mining-off-papua-new-guinea-has-stirred-up-trouble

28 Dochartaigh, Kerri ní, *Thin Places*, Canongate Books, 2021, p15

29 Blackstock, Michael, quoted in Christian, D. and Wong, R. (eds), p43

30 Christian, D. and Wong, R. (eds), *Downstream: Reimagining Water*, Wilfrid Laurier University Press, Waterloo, 2017, p2

Chapter 2. Flow

1 Nakamura, J. and Csikszentmihalyi, M., "The Concept of Flow", *Flow and the Foundations of Positive Psychology*, Springer, 2014, pp239–263

2 Ancestral movement expert Simon Thakur: *ancestralmovement.com*

3 Nadeau, Denise quoted in Christian, D. and Wong, R. (eds), p125
4 Salami, Minna, *Sensuous Knowledge*, Zed Books, 2020
5 Leon, Alannah Young and Nadeau, Denise quoted in Christian, D. and Wong, R. (eds), p135
6 Christian, D. and Wong, R. (eds), p7
7 Water in Biology, waterinbiology.blogspot.com
8 Marlo Fisken, talk at Embodied Trauma conference, 2020
9 Dances for Solidarity, www.dancesforsolidarity.org

Chapter 3. Ebb

1 Dochartaigh, Kerri ní, p23
2 Armitage, Kimo quoted in McCabe, Chris (ed.) *Poems from the Edge of Extinction*, Chambers, 2021
3 Carson, Rachel, *The Sea Around Us*, Oxford University Press, 1951, p71
4 Gibson, Margaret and Frost, Mardi quoted in "Paddle-out: the origins of the surfers memorial circle", *Surfer Today*, 2020, www.surfertoday.com/surfing/paddle-out-the-origins-of-the-surfers-memorial-circle
5 Turner, Toko-pa, *Belonging*, Her Own Room Press, 2017, p122
6 Shulman, Lisa, *Before and After Loss*, Johns Hopkins University Press, 2018
7 Calidas, Tamsin, "Reading *I Am an Island*: Film and Reading", Instagram post, 7 August 2021
8 Buckingham, Lisa, "How cold water swimming helped me cope with the death of my mother", *Red*, 30 January 2021, www.redonline.co.uk/health-self/self/a30699547/cold-water-swimming-benefits/
9 Caddick et al, "The effects of surfing and the natural environment on the well-being of combat veterans", *Qualitative Health Research*, 25(1), 2015, 76-86, p80
10 Caddick et al, 2015, p81
11 Bergland, Christopher, "'Surf Therapy' and Being in the Ocean Can Alleviate PTSD", *Psychology Today*, 28 May 2015, www.psychologytoday.com/ie/blog/the-athletes-way/201505/surf-therapy-and-being-in-the-ocean-can-alleviate-ptsd
12 "Ocean therapy: Finding peace on the water", *RNLI*, 7 November 2019, rnli.org/magazine/magazine-featured-

list/2019/november/ocean-therapy

13 Maté, Gabor, *When the Body Says No*, Vermilion, 2019

14 Elm~~ ~~lwad quoted in an interview with *Vogue*, 2019, www.vogue.com/article/ilwad-elman-interview

15 Elman, Ilwad quoted in an interview with *High Snobeity*, 2020, www.highsnobiety.com/p/ilwad-elman-daily-paper/

16 Marshall, Jamie, "A global exploration of programme theory within surf therapy", unpublished PhD Thesis, Napier University, 2021

17 Elman, Ilwad quoted in an interview with *Vice*, 2018, www.vice.com/en/article/a3nk4j/this-activist-uses-surfing-therapy-to-rehabilitate-child-soldiers

Chapter 4. Mystery

1 Tounouga, Camille Talkeu, "The Symbolic Function of Water in Sub-Saharan Africa: A Cultural Approach", *The MIT Press*, 36, 2003, p283

2 Houston, James, "The Goddess of the Sea: The Story of Sedna", 2015, www.thecanadianencyclopedia.ca/en/article/the-goddess-of-the-sea-the-story-of-sedna

3 Thompson, Nainoa, quoted in Davis, Wade, *The Wayfinders*, House of Anansi Press, 2009, p35

4 Davis, Wade, *The Wayfinders*, House of Anansi Press, 2009, p35

5 Davis, Wade, p53

6 Sea Tamagotchi project, 2020, www.manchan.com/sea-tamagotchi

7 Heke, 2014, p7

8 Cross, Dorothy, *Connemara*, Artisan House, 2013, p98

9 Carson, Rachel, *The Sea Around Us*, Oxford University Press, 1951, p71

10 Giggs, Rebecca, *Fathoms: The World in the Whale*, Simon and Schuster, 2020

11 Kimmerer, Robin Wall, *Braiding Sweetgrass*, Milkweed Editions, 2013, p299

Chapter 5. Power

1 Save the Blue Heart of Europe, www.balkanrivers.net/
2 Bas, "Fighting for Fish to Swim Freely", *World Fish Migration Foundation*, January 2021, worldfishmigrationfoundation. com/fighting-for-fish-to-swim-freely/
3 Urquhart, Julie et al (eds), *Social Issues in Sustainable Fisheries Management*, Springer, 2014, pp143–164
4 Borunda, Alejandra, "Climate Change is Roasting the Himalaya Region, Threatening Millions", *National Geographic*, 4 February 2019, www.nationalgeographic.com/environment/article/himalaya-mountain-climate-change-report
5 Borunda, Alejandra, 2019
6 Wester, Philippus et al, *The Hindu Kush Himalaya Assessment*, Springer, 2019
7 "Why Dams Won't Solve Water Supply Needs", *American Rivers*, 2021, www.americanrivers.org/threats-solutions/restoring-damaged-rivers/dams-wont-solve-water-needs/
8 Derrick, Jensen, Keith, Lierre and Wilbert, Max, "Bright Green Lies", in Hunt et al (eds), *Dark Mountain: Issue 20 – Abyss*, TJ Books, 2021, p202
9 Grill, Günther et al, "Mapping the world's free-flowing rivers", *Nature*, 569(755), 2019, pp215–221
10 WHO and UNICEF Joint Monitoring Programme for Water Supply and Sanitation, "Progress on Drinking Water and Sanitation", *WHO Press*, Geneva, 2014
11 Water Quality and Wastewater, *UN Water Factsheet*, 2021, www.unwater.org/water-facts/quality-and-wastewater
12 Denchak, Melissa, "Water Pollution: Everything You Need to Know", *NRDC*, 18 April 2022, www.nrdc.org/stories/water-pollution-everything-you-need-know
13 Clark, Anna, *The Poisoned City*, Metropolitan Books, 2018
14 Ellis, Erle C et al, "People have shaped most of terrestrial nature for at least 12,000 years", *Proceedings of the National Academy of Sciences*, 118(17), 2021
15 Green, Christie, "Blood Bone Oil Water", in Hunt et al (eds), *Dark Mountain: Issue 20 – Abyss*, TJ Books, 2021, p180
16 Jensen et al, 2021
17 Sturdevant, Molly, "Future Mountains", in Hunt et al (eds), *Dark Mountain: Issue 20 – Abyss*, TJ Books, 2021, p49

18 Maté, Gabor, in conversation with Stephen Porges during the Wisdom of Trauma Conference, 2021

19 Mohawk, John, cited in Christian, D. and Wong, R. (eds), *Downstream*, Wilfrid Laurier University Press, 2017

20 Sharpe, Christina, *In the Wake*, Duke University Press, 2016, quoted in Braverman and Johnson, p10

21 Braverman and Johnson, 2020, p10

22 Dabiri, Emma, *What White People Can Do Next*, Penguin Books, 2021, p62

23 Beresford-Kroeger, Diana, *To Speak for the Trees*, Timber Press, 2019

24 Smith, Anna V., "The Klamath River Now Has the Legal Rights of a Person", *High Country News*, 24 Sept 2019, www.hcn.org/issues/51.18/tribal-affairs-the-klamath-river-now-has-the-legal-rights-of-a-person

25 Hillman, Annelia, in *Guardians of the River* (video), www.outsideonline.com/video/klamath-river-yurok-tribe-dam-removal/

26 Kimmerer, Robin Wall, *Braiding Sweetgrass: Indigenous Wisdom, Scientific Knowledge and the Teachings of Plants*, Milkweed Editions, 2013, p328

27 Kimmerer, 2013, p382

28 Law of the Rights of Mother Earth, Law 071 (2010), Bolivia; Framework Law of Mother Earth and Integral Development for Living Well, Law 300 (2012), Bolivia

29 World Water Law, https://www.codes.earth/waterlaw

30 Leonard, Kelsey, "Why lakes and rivers should have the same rights as humans", *TED Talk*, 2019, www.ted.com/speakers/kelsey_leonard

31 Goldman Environmental Prize for the "Brave Women of Kruščica", Press Release, 2021, balkanrivers.net/en/news/goldman-environmental-prize-for-the-brave-women-of-kruscica

32 Rhiannon Tereariʻi Chandler-ʻIao interview, quoted in Waiwai Ola Waterkeepers Hawaiian Islands, waterkeepershi.org/

33 Indigenous Message on Water: A report from the Indigenous World Forum on Water and Peace, 2014, p19, waterandpeace.files.wordpress.com/2012/07/web_Indigenous-message-on-water_in-web-def.pdf

Chapter 6. Rising

1   Special Report on the Ocean and the Cryosphere in a Changing World, *IPCC*, 2019, www.ipcc.ch/srocc/
2   Macfarlane, Robert, *Underland*, Hamish Hamilton, 2019, p337
3   Neimanis, Astrida, "Held in Suspense: Mustard Gas Legalities in the Gotland Deep", in Braverman, Irus and Johnson, Elizabeth R. (eds), *Blue Legalities*, Duke University Press, 2020, p45
4   Neimanis, 2020, p43
5   O'Toole, Fintan, "Do We Love Ireland Enough to Look After It?" *Irish Times*, 10 July 2021
6   Water Quality in 2020: An Indicators Report, Environmental Protection Agency (EPA), Wexford, 2021
7   Magan, Manchán, *Thirty-two Words for Field*, Gill Books, 2020, p77
8   University of Leeds, "Greenland ice losses rising faster than expected", *Science Daily*, 10 December 2019, www.sciencedaily.com/releases/2019/12/191210111701.htm
9   Bradley, James, "The End of the Oceans", *The Monthly*, 2018, www.themonthly.com.au/issue/2018/august/1533045600/james-bradley/end-oceans
10 Ronda, James P., "Lewis & Clark among the Indians: Down the Columbia", *Journals of the Lewis & Clark Expedition*, 1984, lewisandclarkjournals.unl.edu/item/lc.sup.ronda.01.07
11 Buck, Holly Jean, "Climate Engineering Doesn't Stop Ocean Acidification: Addressing Harms to Ocean Life in Geoengineering Imaginaries", in Braverman, Irus and Johnson, Elizabeth R. (eds), *Blue Legalities*, Duke University Press, 2020, p295
12 The Ocean and Climate Change, *International Union for Conservation of Nature Issues Brief*, IUCN, 2017, www.iucn.org/resources/issues-brief/ocean-and-climate-change
13 Siegel, Seth, *Troubled Water*, Thomas Dunne Books, 2019, p?
14 Roberts, Alli Gold, "Predicting the Future of Global Water Stress", *MIT News*, 9 January 2012
15 Magnason, Andri Snaer, *On Time and Water*, Open Letter, 2021, p67
16 Buck, 2020, p295
17 Horcajo, Kainoa, quoted in *Wai Wai: The Value of Hawaiian Water* (video), 2019
18 The Ice Stupa Project, icestupa.org/

19 Ibrahim, Hindou Oumarou, "Indigenous Knowledge Meets Science to Take on Climate Change", *TEDWomen*, 2019, www.ted.com/talks/hindou_oumarou_ibrahim_Indigenous_ knowledge_meets_science_to_take_on_climate_change

20 Solnit, Rebecca, *Field Guide to Getting Lost,* Canongate Books, 2005, p169

21 Irland, Basia, "Receding/Reseeding", in Hunt et al (eds), *Dark Mountain: Issue 20 – Abyss,* TJ Books, 2021

22 "Aboriginal Women, Water and Health: Reflections from Eleven First Nations, Inuit, and Métis Grandmothers", *Atlantic Centre of Excellence for Women's Health and Prairie Women's Health Centre of Excellence,* 2010, p17

23 Anonymous, "3-day ceremonial walk underway to protest cold lake spill", *CBC News,* 27 October 2013, www.cbc.ca/ news/canada/edmonton/3-day-ceremonial-walk-underway-to-protest-cold-lake-spill-1.2253076

24 Wong, Rita, "Ethical Waters: Reflections on the Healing Walk in the Tar Sands", *Feminist Review* (103), 2013, p133

25 Jetñil-Kijiner, Kathy and Niviâna, Aka, *Rise: From One Island to Another* (poem and video), 2018, 350.org/rise-from-one-island-to-another/

26 Jetñil-Kijiner, Kathy, *New Year New Monsters and New Poems,* 2018, www.kathyjetnilkijiner.com/new-year-new-monsters-and-new-poems/

Chapter 7. Heart

1 Virtue, Doreen, quoted in Ryrie, *The Healing Energies of Water,* Gaia, 1998, pp221–222

2 Neimanis, 2020, p43

3 "Climate Change 2022: Impacts, Adaptation and Vulnerability", *IPCC 6th Assessment Report,* 2022, www.ipcc.ch/report/ar6/wg2/

4 Burtscher, Martina and Britton, Easkey, "'There Was Some Kind of Energy Coming into My Heart': Creating Safe Spaces for Sri Lankan Women and Girls to Enjoy the Wellbeing Benefits of the Ocean", *International Journal of Environmental Research and Public Health* 19(6), 2022, p342

5 Romero, Jordyn (director): *We Are Like Waves,* 2021

6 Giggs, Rebecca, *Fathoms,* Simon and Schuster, 2020

7 Skerry, Brian, "Oceanic Discoveries" panel session at UN World Oceans Day, 8 June 2021, unworldoceansday.org/un-

world-oceans-day-2021/

8 The Algonquin Water Song, www.singthewatersong.com/
   songlyrics

9 Andry, Nancy quoted in *Singing the Water Song*,
   www.singthewatersong.com/songlyrics

10 "Aboriginal Women, Water and Health", report, 2010, p21

11 Starhawk, "Waters of the World", In: Emoto, M (Ed) *The
   Healing Power of Water*, 2004, p177

12 Neimanis, 2020, p11

13 Buck, 2020, p306

14 Christian and Wong, 2017, p6

15 Carson, Liam, "Tearmann: Sanctuary", *New Hibernia Review*
   9(3), 2005, pp9–16

Cultivating Ebb and Flow

1 Juster-Horsfield, Hope H., and Bell, Sarah L., "Supporting
   'blue care' through outdoor water-based activities:
   practitioner perspectives", *Qualitative Research in Sport,
   Exercise and Health* 14(1), 2022, p137–150

FURTHER RESOURCES

Books

Akomolafe, Bayo, *These Wilds Beyond Our Fences*, North Atlantic Books, 2017

Beresford-Kroeger, Diana, *To Speak for the Trees*, Timber Press, 2019

Bleakley, Sam, *Mindful Thoughts for Surfers*, Leaping Hare Press, 2020

Braverman, Irus and Johnson, Elizabeth R (eds), *Blue Legalities*, Duke University Press, 2020

Britton, Easkey, *Saltwater in the Blood*, Watkins, 2021

Britton, Easkey, *50 Things to Do by the Sea*, Pavilion, 2021

Carson, Rachel, *The Sea Around Us*, Oxford University Press, 1991 (first published 1951)

Christian, D and Wong, R (eds), *Downstream*, Wilfrid Laurier University Press, 2017

Earle, Sylvia, *Sea Change*, Ballantine Books, 1995

Foley, Ronan et al (eds), *Blue Space, Health and Wellbeing*, Routledge, 2020

Giggs, Rebecca, *Fathoms*, Simon and Schuster, 2020

Goodell, Jeff, *The Water Will Come*, Little, Brown, 2017

Gooley, Tristan, *How to Read Water*, Sceptre, 2016

Harper, Mark, *Chill*, Chronicle Books, 2022

Hill, Lauren, *She Surf*, Gestalten, 2020

Hoare, Philip, *The Sea Inside*, Fourth Estate, 2014

Johnson, Ayana Elizabeth and Wilkinson, Katherine (eds), *All We Can Save*, One World, 2020

Jones, Lucy, *Losing Eden*, Allen Lane, 2020

Kelly, Catherine, *Blue Spaces*, Welbeck Balance, 2021

Kimmerer, Robin Wall, *Braiding Sweetgrass*, Milkweed Editions, 2013

Lindstrom, Carole, *We Are Water Protectors*, Roaring Book Press, 2020

Loewe, Emma, *Return to Nature*, HarperOne, 2022

Magan, Manchán, *Listen to the Land Speak*, Gill Books, 2022

Magnason, Andri Snaer, *On Time and Water*, Open Letter, 2021

Maté, Gabor, *The Myth of Normal*, Vermilion, 2022

Macfarlane, Robert, *Underland*, Hamish Hamilton, 2019

Neruda, Pablo, *On the Blue Shores of Silence*, HarperCollins, 2004

Nichols, Wallace J, *Blue Mind*, Little, Brown and Company, 2014

Nicolson, Adam, *The Seabird's Cry*, William Collins, 2018

Stephen W. Porges, *The Polyvagal Theory*, W. W. Norton & Company, 2011

Runcie, Charlotte, *Salt on Your Tongue*, Canongate, 2020

Rush, Elizabeth, *Rising*, Milkweed Editions, 2018

Ryrie, Charlie, *The Healing Energies of Water*, Gaia, 1998

Salami, Minna, *Sensuous Knowledge*, Zed Books, 2020

Solnit, Rebecca, *A Paradise Built in Hell*, Viking Press, 2009

Strang, Veronica, *Water*, Reaction Books, 2015

Tsui, Bonnie, *Why We Swim*, Algonquin Books, 2020

Whitworth, Victoria, *Swimming with Seals*, Head of Zeus, 2017

Online Resources

Blue health
BlueHealth: bluehealth2020.eu
Inclusea: inclusea.eu
Moving Oceans: movingoceans.com
River Listening Project: www.riverlistening.com.au
Saltwater Songlines: www.saltwatersonglines.com
Seas Oceans and Public Health in Europe (SOPHIE):
 sophie2020.eu
We Are Ocean: weareocean.blue

Blue care initiatives
Beyond the Surface International:
 www.beyondthesurfaceinternational.org
Changing Tides Foundation:
 www.changingtidesfoundation.org
Groundswell Community Project:
 www.groundswellcommunity.org
I Am Water Foundation: www.iamwaterfoundation.org
International Surf Therapy Organization: intlsurftherapy.org
Liquid Therapy: www.liquidtherapy.ie
Native Like Water: www.nativelikewater.org
SeaSisters: www.seasisterslk.com
UNESCO Ocean Literacy: oceanliteracy.unesco.org

Water protection resources
All We Can Save Project: www.allwecansave.earth
Fair Seas: fairseas.ie
Guardians of the River: www.riverguardians.co
Oceanic Global: oceanic.global
Ocean Justice Forum: www.oceanjusticeforum.info
Open Rivers: openrivers.eu
Save the Blue Heart of Europe: blueheart.patagonia.
 com/discover
Save the Waves: www.savethewaves.org

The Mega Lab: www.themegalab.org
United Nations Ocean Decade: www.oceandecade.org
Water Keeper Alliance: waterkeeper.org
Water Justice Hub: www.waterjusticehub.org
We Are One Ocean: www.weareoneocean.org
World Water Law: www.codes.earth/waterlaw

ACKNOWLEDGEMENTS

My deep and abiding gratitude to the constancy of the ocean and wild water bodies that supported the creative process of writing this book, especially for the ebb and flow that allowed me to find the spaces between the waves to write. This story is shaped by the seen and unseen forces of water. And by the incredible forces of love in my life.

Both my parents are present in this book. Thanks to my mother, who has always found a way to encourage and support me in everything I've ever done. Her therapeutic work with women influenced my emphasis on the healing potential of water, especially for women. My father, for passing on his deep love of the sea and creative expression. Beckey-Finn, my sister, for sharing her grace, grit and gratitude with me over all the years. Aurora, for reminding us all of the simple joy of being, to be present with what is. My grandmother, for teaching me the sacredness water.

Neil, my partner and fellow surfer, supported this book by making sure I got plenty of water time – knowing this is where I soak up the most inspiration, helping me to reconnect with what matters most, listening to my wild ideas and his unquestioning respect for my need to get away to edge-places sometimes. Barra and Fianna, allowing me to love more deeply than I ever imagined possible.

In the process of writing this book I discovered the beautiful, rich web of relationships with my water kin, human and non-human – the friendships, inspiration, mentorship and guidance in my life – was revealed. In particular, all those adventurers, artists, water lovers and researchers who have inspired me and generously given their time sharing their water wisdom with me, either for this project or at various points in my life: Aka Niviâna, Anne Byrne, Caitriona Lynch, Cliff Kapono, Connor Ryan, Dorothy Cross, Hanli Prinsloo, Ihi Heke, Sofia Casal Silva, Ruth Le Gear, Ilwad Elman, Jamie Marshall, Martina Burtscher and the pioneering female surfers of Iran and Sri Lanka, Melissa Reid, Pat McCabe, Sarah Bell and Starma. Thank you Ayana Elizabeth Johnson, Bonnie Tsui, Elizabeth Rush, Kerri ní Dochartaigh, Manchán Magan, Robin Wall Kimmerer, Tamsin Calidas, Wallace J Nichols and all those writers who help give voice to our watery relationships, inspiring me to find my own voice.

I'm grateful to the small island communities, especially Inishturk and Inishbofin, who always make me feel welcome and at ease in my own skin, I thank you. To the keepers of Fanad Lighthouse, thank you for inviting me to the most spectacular place to write.

Ebb and Flow would not have been possible without my wonderful publisher Fiona Robertson for her belief in the power of this story and to all the team at Watkins Publishing for taking this book from idea to reality, especially assistant editor Brittany Willis, copyeditor Victoria Goldman, designer Karen Smith, Laura Whitaker-Jones and her incredible marketing team. Thanks also to my supportive agent David McHugh and my publicist Helen at Gill Hess for all her encouragement.

I would like to thank the Water Protectors, all those whose lives are in service to water. Lastly, I'm grateful for my muses – the rugged coast of Donegal, Atlantic ocean swells, kelp forests, fulmar, salmon, seal and shark.

ABOUT THE AUTHOR

Dr Easkey Britton is a marine social scientist, writer, artist and ocean leader, with a deep love and passion for surfing and the sea. Her work explores the relationship between people and nature, especially water environments. She contributes her expertise in blue space, health and social wellbeing on national and international research projects.

A life-long surfer, her parents taught her to surf when she was four years old and she channels her passion for surfing and the sea into social change. Her work is deeply influenced by the ocean and the lessons learned pioneering women's big wave surfing in Ireland. Her ground-breaking journey to Iran in 2013 introduced the sport of surfing to women and local communities and is featured in the award-winning documentary film *Into the Sea*. Easkey facilitates international leadership programmes specializing in experiential learning, nature connection, embodiment practices, community engagement and social impact.

She is the author of *Saltwater in the Blood* and *50 Things to Do by the Sea*, has published numerous peer-reviewed journal articles and is a regular columnist with *Oceanographic* magazine. She currently lives on the west coast of Ireland with her family.